PENJING:
THE CHINESE ART
OF BONSAI

PENJING
THE CHINESE ART OF BONSAI

A Pictorial Exploration of
Its History, Aesthetics, Styles and Preservation

ZHAO QINGQUAN

Better Link Press

Managing Directors: Wang Youbu, Xu Naiqing
Executive Editors: Zhang Yicong, Yang Xiaohe, Susan Luu Xiang
Assistant Editor: Jiang Danting

Text: Zhao Qingquan
Photographs: Zhao Qingquan (Yangzhou, Jiangsu Province), Wu Chengfa (Hong Kong), Huang Le (Yangzhou, Jiangsu Province), Han Xuenian (Shunde, Guangdong Province), Zheng Yongtai (Qingyuan, Guangdong Province) and Rui Xinhua (Nanjing, Jiangsu Province)
Translation: Jiang Yajun, Ma Suping

Cover Design Consultant: Diane Davies
Design: Yuan Yinchang, Li Jing, Zhong Yiming

ISBN: 978-1-60220-009-8

Address any comments about *Penjing: The Chinese Art of Bonsai—A Pictorial Exploration of Its History, Aesthetics, Styles and Preservation* to:

Shanghai Press and Publishing Development Co., Ltd.
Floor 5, No. 390 Fuzhou Road, Shanghai, China (200001)
Email: sppd@sppdbook.com

Printed in China by Shanghai Donnelley Printing Co., Ltd.

5   7   9   10   8   6

CONTENTS

序言 | FOREWORD

It is a great pleasure to introduce *Penjing: The Chinese Art of Bonsai—A Pictorial Exploration of Its History, Aesthetics, Styles and Preservation* by Zhao "Brook" Qingquan. An astounding accomplishment, this book stands among the world's premier volumes on the true art of Chinese penjing. Reading the text, it is as if we have entered into some sort of magical machine that can transcend time and distance, revealing secrets of the ancient art; some from over 600 years ago and from the cultural heart of China.

The wonderful and comprehensive material in this book fills a huge void in the global bonsai scene. It can truly alter the western point of view towards this living art. As Brook explains the concept of penjing subsumes bonsai and includes tree penjing, landscape penjing, and water and land penjing. So while the west uses a Japanese word, bonsai, to define the art, the penjing approach can be so much more. The depth and richness of Chinese culture towards all penjing as explained in the following pages will truly astound and leave you clamoring for more.

Beyond the detailed historical information, Brook holds a lofty position as one of the world's foremost masters of penjing, and he reveals much of his approach here. Covering the aesthetics of penjing through to the actual practical technique, to a detailed discussion of popular tree species in China, this book shines. The gorgeous layout, excellent photography of the creative penjing, and crisp, clear writing make the book a joy to read. Throughout, Brook deftly relates the penjing concepts to various Chinese cultural references and as such gives the reader an amazing view into the grandness of Chinese culture and tradition. This type of information will imbue the reader with a freshness sure to enhance your appreciation and perhaps practice of penjing. I know after reading it I was energized to work on a penjing and I'm sure you will be too.

Robert Kempinski
President
Bonsai Clubs International
USA

(facing page)
Gorgeous Glow
Species: *Acer palmatum* (Japanese Maple)
Height of tree: 115 cm
Age of tree: 50 years
Container: Oval glazed pottery tray
Designers: Zhao Qingquan & Zhou Qijin
Introduction: With arresting red leaves and vigorous branches, the Japanese Maple penjing in a yellowish oval glazed pottery tray features the gorgeous scene of maples in autumn. The leaves are removed in the late summer for fresh new red ones, which come out in about two weeks.

Dancer
Species: *Sabina procumbens* (Creeping Juniper)
Age of tree: 55 years old
Height of tree: 42 cm
Container: Rectangular sandy clay tray
Designer: Zhao Qingquan
Introduction: Carefully select the front of a tree. With the longer primary branches progressing to the left, the penjing work resembles a dancer in a traditional Chinese long-sleeve style dress.

前言 | PREFACE

Originated in China, bonsai (*penzai*) is a living art form using miniature trees grown in containers (pots or trays), along with shaped rockeries and other materials, to create aesthetic representations of natural landscapes. The craft was brought to Japan in the Southern Song dynasty of China (1127–1279), or the late Heian period in Japan (794–1192). It has now reached a worldwide audience ever since the art form was introduced to the West from Japan in modern times.

Chinese penjing, literally means "tray/pot scenery," are small-scale artistic renditions of natural landscapes by artistic orchestrations of carefully pruned trees, rocks, soil and water. As an art aiming at "seeing the big from the tiny," it is often created as a method of self-expression to convey personal emotions. In China, bonsai is one of the three categories of penjing and is known as *shumu penjing* or "tree penjing," with the other two being *shanshui penjing* or "landscape penjing" and *shuihan penjing* or "water and land penjing."

While tree penjing depicts in containers the images of natural trees and plants, its dominant elements in the composition are wired, pruned and chiseled to create aesthetic images; landscape penjing specimens feature landscapes of islands and mountains by cutting, engraving and reshaping carefully chosen rocks, usually in contact with water and decorated with small live plants. A third category, water and land penjing, is a blend of the previous two types, depicting a more "complete" picture of a scene–not only a landscape consisting of mountains and water, but also the images of tree and plants. The source materials may include plants, rocks, soil, water and, if necessary, miniatures.

As an integrated form of art, penjing is an extension of garden art, but with the help of devices and techniques from painting, sculpture, poetry and pottery making, among others.

The penjing artist seeks a balance between the beauty of nature and the beauty of art. The major source materials are natural, and the trees and plants grow and change with the seasons. Penjing, therefore, is an art with life.

Just as landscape art allows the viewers to appreciate in a small space an expanse of scenery, the size of penjing allows them to do the same before a small tray or pot. A penjing specimen is therefore a mini-garden, but in a more compact fashion.

Penjing aesthetics emphasizes *huayi* and *shiqing*, or "(ink) painting flavor" and "poetic image." The former focuses on the design of penjing resembling that of a Chinese traditional ink painting, which features its function in capturing the essence and spirit of a natural landscape through abstraction to keep a balance between art and nature. To achieve this goal, rather than to strive for a photographic reproduction of a natural scene, the artist needs to maintain a balance between dominance and subordination, emptiness (void) and substance, denseness and sparseness, highness and lowness, largeness and smallness, life and death, dynamics and statics, roughness and meticulousness, firmness and gentleness, lightness and darkness, straightness and curviness, verticality and horizontality and lightness and heaviness. The main task of the artist is to balance varied forces against each other to attain equilibrium.

The latter, "poetic image," means that while reminiscent of their full-size counterparts in the wild, penjing specimens evoke associations and stimulates the mind, allowing the viewer to go beyond the mere landscape that they are enjoying to convey personal feelings of their affections, wishes and ideals.

Human beings are born with the desire of being

(facing page)

Full Bloom
Species: *Malus spectabilis* (Chinese Flowering Crabapple)
Age of tree: 60 years old
Height of tree: 56 cm
Container: Oval glazed pottery tray
Designer: Zhao Qingquan
Introduction: The Chinese Flowering Crabapple is a graceful species for both its beautiful flowers in the spring and its fruits in the autumn and winter. This specimen has a natural crown with dynamic movements of the trunk and branches. It produces gorgeous flowers in the spring.

Sailing out of Three Gorges
Type of rock: Limestone
Container: Marble tray
Length of container: 100 cm
Designer: Rui Xinhua
Introduction: Benefiting greatly from the techniques of Chinese splash-ink painting, the work portrays the lofty mountains and high ranges in the Three Gorges in China's Yangtze River using natural shapes of the rocks. The penjing is placed in a round tray to show the depth of the scene.

(facing page)

Life in Sparse Forest
Species: *Serissa foetita* (Snowrose)
Age of (main) tree: 20 years old
Type of rock: Turtle Shell Rock
Container: Rectangular marble tray
Length of container: 90 cm
Designer: Zhao Qingquan
Introduction: Snowroses have small foliage with small leaves but an aged look. Several snowroses of various sizes and Turtle Shell Rocks are carefully orchestrated to give rise to a highly dynamic composition of a sparse forest. The chess-playing figurines under the trees add much liveliness to the landscape.

close to nature and living a tranquil life. However, many of us suffer from a sense of alienation from our natural environment as we face more and more work and family related pressures because of the increasing pace of industrialization in our modern world. Instead, penjing art allows us to pursue peacefulness and tranquility in our inner hearts and fulfill our desires of being part of nature. It is used to decorate our homes and to cultivate self-expression, helping us achieve a healthier and happier life. In addition, as an art form expressing the human desire to love nature and peace in the world,

it has gained increasing popularity around the globe. Therefore, penjing as an old traditional art has been renewed.

Chinese penjing as a distinctive category of art has been practiced in more and more places in the world. As an introduction to the penjing art, this book covers its concept, history, categories, source trees, techniques, display, and care and maintenance. A nicely illustrated book, it is written for penjing enthusiasts for practical purposes and others who are interested in Chinese culture in general.

Spirit of Daoism
Species: *Fortunella hindsii* (Hong Kong Kumquat)
Age of tree: 30 years old
Type of rock: Ying Rock
Container: Oval sandy clay tray
Length of container: 60 cm
Designer: Wu Chengfa
Introduction: This is a tree-in-rock penjing. The tree was trained in a deep pot, where it developed its long roots. It was created by inserting its roots into the racks and joints of the rocks to feature an old tree firmly rooted in mountain rocks in nature.

14

Striking Energy
Species: *Ulmus parvifolia* (Chinese Elm)
Age of tree: 40 years old
Height of tree: 90 cm
Container: Rectangular sandy clay tray
Designer: Wu Chengfa
Introduction: This literati style penjing with two upright trunks portrays the sense of justice and proud loneliness of traditional Chinese literati. The two contrasting trunks were originally one thicker trunk.

CHAPTER ONE

PENJING AESTHETICS

All good penjing specimens are creations by the joint efforts of the artist and nature. They are artistic re-arrangements of natural materials, featuring a highly appealing blend of nature and art, for which penjing as an art form is appreciated. The artistic beauty of penjing lies in its painted image and poetic image.

Penjing is endowed with an inherent charm, gift and grace due to its use of nature as artistic media. As trees grow with age and seasons change, penjing serves as a reminder of life itself. Therefore, penjing as a work of art is a living sculpture.

As a living art form, penjing building is always a process, rather than a product. Different from other art forms such as painting and sculpture that are finished once for all time, a penjing is always "finished" temporarily and modified later as the tree grows. Specimens that the artist is not satisfied with at present may be his best work years later. The charm of penjing lies partially in the process of the seemingly endless process of revision, which is always filled with anticipation.

Naturalness

With the natural shapes and colors of its main artistic medium–rock, soil, water, growing grasses, vines, plants and trees, penjing is appreciated first and foremost due to the artist's consideration of its intrinsic values.

Much of the naturalness of penjing comes from the incorporation of growing trees and plants: their roots, trunks, branches, leaves, flowers and fruits; their structures and shapes, and their adaptation to seasonal change.

Naturalness of penjing
This is a detail of the penjing named *Quiet Forest* (see page 109 for details). The rocks, soil, and water, with their natural shapes and colors, rhyme with the living trees and plants, and the charm of life permeates every inch of the scene.

Roots. Shapes and locations of tree roots vary enormously by species and growing condition. Some grow deeply in the ground while others have roots that fan out broadly and stay closer to the surface of the soil; some trees have a large taproot that extends straight down from the trunk, while others have tangled roots. In other species, roots work their way into the cracks of rocks.

Trunks. Tree trunks also vary considerably from tree to tree. While some are towering and majestic, others are stunningly vigorous and graceful. Saplings have robust trunks; ancient ones have knotted and gnarled boles. Different species have different trunks. For example, pines are thick and scaly, while crape myrtle have fine and smooth trunks. In terms of color, tree trunks can be dark green, black, grayish brown, red, yellowish brown, or purple black. Some tree trunks are half-dead, leaving

(facing page)
Spirit of Pines
Species: *Pinus massoniana* (Chinese Red Pine)
Height of tree: 140 cm
Container: Rectangular marble tray
Designer: Han Xuenian
Introduction: A perfect composition. This penjing was trained from the stump of a Chinese Red Pine and it has been potted for 15 years. The raised ground around the bottom, the dragon-shaped trunk, the rough bark, and the carefully pruned foliage artistically feature the rigor of an aged pine.

Fascinating roots
This is a detail of an Orange Jasmine penjing. The whorled roots indicate how firmly the tree is standing in the soil.

Magnificent leaves
The rich leaves of the Japanese Maple in the late autumn are glowing red.

Arresting tree trunk
This is a detail of a Sargent's Chinese Juniper penjing. The combination of the dead area, the *sheli* or *shari*, with the contrasting signs of life presented by the vigorous foliage is artistically compelling, making the viewer wonder about the age of the tree.

a stunning contrast between the dead area, called *sheli* in Chinese penjing and *shari* in Japanese bonsai, and growing part of the foliage mass.

Branches. Branches of tree differ wildly in size, shape, strength and texture. Some are straight and strong, others are curvy and flexible. Some trees have large and sparse branches, but others produce foliage with tiny but dense wigs. Some tree branches are like deer-horns, but others resemble crab claws.

Leaves. The leaves of plants exhibit much variation in shape, varying from ovate-oblong to cuneate-obovate, and from needle or scale shape to fan or melon shape. Some plants are with hard leaves, while some produce soft ones; some are with thick leaves, while some produce thin ones. The leaves also vary greatly in color, from light or medium green to deeper greens. Some leaves, being part of flowers, are floral leaves, but others are green with red edges.

Flowers. Depending on the variety, flowers vary even more wildly than leaves in shape as well as color, which is why they are so popular.

Fruits. Fruits are symbols of harvest and reproduction. They come in a variety of shapes and colors, ranging from red and gold to purple and orange to green.

Beauty of trees. Most trees are beautiful compositions of roots, trunk, branches, flowers and fruits in various shapes and colors. Like people, they assume the appearance of maturity as they grow and age.

Seasonal beauty. The allure of trees is their change in shape and color throughout the seasons of the year. This is especially true with many broad-leaved species, whose fresh soft green leaves turn deeper green in summer and yellow in autumn before they drop. When

Seasonal beauty
Red leaves of the Japanese Maple, evergreen foliage of the pine, and yellow crowns of Maidenhair trees are a reminder of late autumn.

Geological beauty
This is a detail of the penjing entitled *An Old Tree over a Pond* (see page 69 for details). The rough ash black of the Turtle Shell Rocks look sedate and decorous.

Beauty in shape
This piece of unpolished natural Turtle Shell Rock with a variety of texture which appear to be created by a technique often used in traditional Chinese landscape painting would lend visual and tactile interest to your penjing composition.

Beauty of colors
This is a detail of the penjing named *Quiet Forest* (see page 109 for details). Mosses are growing on the carefully maintained Turtle Shell Rocks, adding liveliness as well as a painted image to the composition.

the leaves have fallen, the bare branches, sometimes covered with crystal white snow, add great interest to the scene. The seasonal beauty of trees is one of the reasons why penjing is such a gratifying art form all year round.

Other source materials such as rock, soil and water also contribute to the aesthetics of penjing. The solid nature of soil, the dynamics of water, and the shape, texture and color of a rock are all beyond human creation.

The beauty of a rock mainly lies in its quality, shape and color.

Quality. Rocks can be soft and hard, impressing viewers in quite different ways. Lingbi Rock from Lingbi in Anhui Province, Ying Rock from Yingde in Guangdong Province, silicified wood and cobblestone are among the hardest rock types. Second to them are Turtle Shell Rock and Stalagmite Rock. Reed tube stone and sandstone are soft in nature.

Shape. Rocks are used in penjing mainly for their shape and markings. A piece of rock may look like a peak, range or river bank. The markings on rocks vary greatly from one category to another. An ideal rock has a variety of textures that give visual and tactile interest to a penjing composition.

Color. Rocks may be of various colors, from yellowish brown to grayish blue and white. Rocks of different colors are incorporated in different penjing scenes to add particular interest.

Design

The aesthetic shape of penjing is one of the most important criteria by which a design is judged. Through the shaping process, painted images are created in penjing.

A penjing is a three-dimensional landscape painting that is created with media from nature, though the scene is never designed as an exact replica of nature. Rather, it is always a re-creation of natural landscapes or trees with a touch of abstraction.

Traditional Chinese painting can be compared to the human body; rocks is the skeleton, water is the blood and trees is the skin. It is often said that in a painting "water gives mountains life, and rocks are vitalized by trees," or that "immovable mountains are animated by running water, and trees give life to motionless rocks." Penjing art and traditional Chinese landscape painting share the same principles in composition design. While the former is three-dimensional, they are both artistic re-creations of natural landscapes that aspire to capture the inherent beauty of nature.

The following guidelines are essential in shaping a penjing:

Dominance and subordination. There can only be one component that dominates all the others in a composition. However, there is always a leading ingredient in a visibly independent section. Techniques are needed to highlight dominant features to better represent your theme, and to help the viewer to focus.

Emptiness and substance. According to traditional Chinese philosophy, the world is a blend of emptiness and substance that are created by each other and reside in each other. To represent the essence and nature of the world in a realistic and dynamic manner, penjing artists should arrange the components so that parts of the composition that have nothing to show (empty space), for example, are balanced by an amount of substance. This encourages the viewer to let his imagination run beyond the mere landscape.

Denseness and sparseness. While a tightly packed landscape may make viewers feel nervous and even depressed, one that is too sparse feels loose and shapeless like an oversized t-shirt. As every piece of artwork possesses its own inner rhythms, spacing techniques help highlight the contrasts between facets of the design of a penjing specimen, imbuing it with life and music. The balance between denseness and sparseness gives the impression of a forest from just a couple of miniature trees.

Roughness and meticulousness. The best penjing specimens maintain a balance between roughness and meticulousness. The arrangement of a penjing usually starts with its overall layout, rather than the details of individual components and complementary features, which can only be taken into account when the artist is satisfied with the layout. This helps to give him a sense of entirety, which decides in what manner the theme is represented.

Firmness and gentleness. Nature in its entirety is varied but harmonious, where well kept landscapes are a balance between firmness and gentleness. Such relation in a penjing can be reflected in its theme, style, shape and source materials. However, one can never be pursued at the cost of the others, because they complement each other to form a varied but cohesive whole.

Entirety and individuality. The components in penjing–tree, rock, water, land mass and miniature–are never isolated items but are chosen with an eye toward their ability to contribute to the whole design. The sense of interrelation is usually represented in movements, categories, shapes, lines and colors of the components. The entire composition is composed by individual components.

The beauty of a composition is also reflected in how tall, large, straight and upright the components are and whether the landscape varies in form, dynamics and openness. All these seemingly contradictory relations are unities of opposites.

Waiting for a Phoenix
Species: *Sageretia theezans*
(Chinese Bird Plum)
Age of tree: 80 years old
Height of tree: 100 cm
Container: Rectangular marble
tray
Designer: Wu Chengfa
Introduction: This aged
Chinese Bird Plum has flowing
lines. The long primary
branch protruding from the
foliage rhymes with the old
appearance of the trunk, adding
a dynamic feature to the whole
composition to reveal the
vigorous and imposing manner.

21

Green Cloud
Species: *Juniperus chinensis* var. *sargentii* (Sargent's Chinese Juniper)
Age of tree: 60 years old
Height of tree: 115 cm
Container: Chinese-crabapple-shaped sandy clay pot
Designer: Bao Shiqi
Introduction: This is a *sheli* style Sargent's Chinese Juniper, lines of living veins running along the dead wood. The foliage is extremely dense, like green clouds, but with a clear sense of denseness and sparseness, featuring a typical natural aged pine.

22

The Milky Way Waterfall
Type of rock: Axe-split Rock
Container: Rectangular marble tray
Length of container: 150 cm
Designer: Qiao Honggen
Introduction: A narrow piece of marble is artistically attached along the hill, making it a waterfall. The work created with colorful Axe-split Rocks as its major medium appears to be created by nature rather than an artist.

23

Species: *Stranvaesia davidiana* (Chinese Stranvaesia)
Age of tree: 80 years old
Height of tree: 123 cm
Designer: Lu Xueming
Container: Square glazed pottery pot
Introduction: This is a shoreline-style water and land penjing, with a beautiful contrast between the two trunks. The branches are pruned into a vigorous deer-horn shape, with a clear sense of denseness and sparseness in the gorgeous foliage shape. This is typical of Lingnan (covering Guangdong and Guangxi provinces) School of penjing.

Skyscaper
Species: *Pinus parviflora*
(Japanese Five Needle Pine)
Age of tree: 60 years old
Height of tree: 100 cm
Designer: Hu Yueguo
Container: Rectangular sandy clay tray
Introduction: This double-trunk penjing with towering trunks and drooping branches represents an old Japanese Five Needle Pine in the wild. The two trunks are closely attached to each other, full of energy; and the clear sense of denseness and sparseness and the balance between emptiness and substance stir the imagination.

25

Autumn Thoughts

Species: *Ulmus parvifolia* (Chinese Elm), *Sageretia theezans* (Chinese Hackberry), *Vitex negundo var. cannabifolia* (Cutleaf Chaste Tree) , *Ligustrum obtusifolium* (Border Privet) and *Acer buergerianum* (Trident Maple)

Container: Oval glazed pottery tray

Length of container: 50 cm

Designer: He Gansun

Introduction: Image, an important part in understanding traditional Chinese aesthetics, is one of the most important criteria by which a design is judged. The components in a composition are imbued with the artist's affection for nature. This enables him to go beyond the limited landscape to create an artistically unlimited scene in a small container. An old tree or several pieces of rock, for example, stirs the imagination. This specimen portrays the image of *Autumn Thoughts* by Ma Zhiyuan (c.1251 – after 1321), a well-known Chinese poet of the Yuan dynasty. The poem goes as follows: A withered vine, an ancient tree, crows at dusk/ A little bridge, a flowing stream, some huts/ An old road, wind out of the west, an emaciated horse/ A heart-broken man on the horizon at sunset.

Image

"Image" is an important term in understanding traditional Chinese aesthetics. Like Chinese landscape painting, landscape poetry and landscape gardening, the ultimate goal in Chinese penjing as a literati art is in pursuing the image of beauty. The components in a composition are imbued with the artist's unique view of the world and his love for nature. This enables the viewer to see beyond the limited landscape to capture their imagination and emotions.

Poetic image. A penjing artist and a landscape poet share the goal of communicating with others by enrooting their own feelings into scenes. Just as the several lines in a poem express much more between them, the penjing artist strives to convey boundless meaning with miniature trees and pieces of rocks in a small container.

Unity of boldness and restraint. The images of penjing can be forceful, bold, restrained or delicate. Like garden art, penjing's dynamic touch is in the quiet scenes, which appears to be pleasant and relaxing. Boldness and restraint should co-exist in penjing and complement each other.

Symbolism. Symbolism and association are methods commonly used in creating images in penjing design. The generations of Chinese literati bestowed specific symbolic meanings to things in nature. While a rock symbolizes eternity, water is full of intelligence and trees reveal human characteristics. These symbolic meanings, understood by the artist and the viewer, provide better insight to the poetic images and associations.

Inscription. Couplets are hung on columns of a hall in a Chinese garden and banners are placed above the gates, and a poem is often brushed on a Chinese painting. In a similar fashion, a short and concise title is often composed for poetic effect and artistic flair to go with the theme and image that the artist is trying to project.

Images stimulate the mind, and it allows us to look at a piece over and over again with fresh eyes, always discovering a new aspect but never feeling satiated.

Image in Liu Songnian
Species: *Pinus parviflora* (Japanese Five Needle Pine)
Age of tree: 85 years old
Height of tree: 110 cm
Container: Rectangular stone tray
Designer: Pan Zhonglian
Introduction: This work uses Southern Song dynasty painter Liu Songnian's painting image to represent the imposing grandeur and energy of natural Japanese Five Needle Pines. The trunks and foliage are trained to show variety in a unified entirety.

(above)

Eight Horses
Species: *Serissa foetita* (Snowrose)
Age of (main) tree: 20 years old
Type of rock: Turtle Shell Rock
Container: Rectangular marble tray
Length of container: 180 cm
Designer: Zhao Qingquan
Introduction: The scene of eight horses has been the subject of many paintings in China. Using the techniques of traditional Chinese painting, the sparse forest, open grassland, calm creek and the horses are carefully orchestrated to complement each other and give rise to a quiet, peaceful, natural and romantic composition in such a long and shallow container. The creek style penjing shows a clear sense of dominance and subordination, and a sharp balance between denseness and sparseness. The sizes of the trees and rocks are in proportion to their locations in the composition. The water surface manages to show the depth of the scene and enhance the locations of relative components.

(left)

Sharp Sense of Integrity
Species: *Juniperus formosana* (Taiwan Juniper)
Age of tree: More than 90 years old
Height of tree: 115 cm
Container: Round sandy clay pot
Designer: Zhao Qingquan
Introduction: The tree in this literati penjing is nearly 100 years old. The drooping primary branch twists along the trunk in a simple but unconventional manner; the twisting branches echo the straight trunk; and the dead part of the trunk, or the *sheli* or *shari*, contrasts with the living veins. The towering trunk and the simple foliage evoke the characteristics of a sharp sense of integrity.

CHAPTER TWO
HISTORY OF PENJING

While its history can be traced back to the Han (206 BC – AD 220) and Jin (265 – 420) dynasties in China, penjing as an art form developed in the Tang dynasty (618 – 907). By the Song (960 – 1279) and Yuan (1279 – 1368) dynasties, the Chinese were already practicing the art at an advanced level. The Ming (1368 – 1644) and Qing (1644 – 1911) dynasties witnessed its peak in popularity before it experienced a decline in the following years. The conditions in China at present have allowed for a renaissance of this ancient art form.

Han and Jin Dynasties

As one of the world's oldest civilizations, China's massive land, varied climates and natural landscapes have long inspired the artistic mind. Three thousand years ago, during the Shang (c.1600 – 1046 BC) and Zhou (1046 – 256 BC) dynasties, ornamental plants were cultivated and miniature landscapes created to pursue "harmony between people and nature." Chinese traditional art was greatly influenced by the principles of Daoism during the Spring and Autumn period (770 – 476 BC) and Warring States period (475 – 221 BC), which proposed turning to nature to discover original order. Relating people's affection for mountains and waters to their different characters, Confucius believed that "the wise enjoy waters; the benevolent enjoy mountains." Legend has it that the Shanglin Garden of the Qin dynasty (221 – 206 BC) covered an area of more than 10,000 square miles and people in Eastern Han dynasty (25 – 220) planted flowers in containers and "collected stones to create miniature mountains."

China's long history of pottery and porcelain making provides great advantages for the production of the container to grow plants, known as the *pen*. It is a vital foundation for penjing. Crude, red pottery containers and vessels were made for daily living from the Neolithic period (c.6000 – 4000 BC) to the Xia (2070 – 1600 BC), Shang and Zhou dynasties, and glazed basins and celadon wares were produced in low-temperature kilns from the Spring and Autumn period and Warring States period to Qin and Han dynasties (221 BC – AD 220). The earliest historical record of a nascent form of penjing is found in the fresco in the entrance hall of an Eastern Han tomb excavated at Wangdu in Hebei Province: six red flower plants arranged in a round container placed on a square frame. This indicates that bonsai as an art form was already part of life in Chinese families 1,900 years ago.

During the years of social turmoil following the Wei (220 – 265) and Jin (265 – 420) dynasties, with the popularity of Buddhism and the influence of the Confucianism and Daoism, people became indifferent to fame and wealth, and many abandoned themselves to nature by practicing a hermit's way of life. To be able to appreciate the beauty of landscapes was part of one's dream of an ideal life. As a result, landscape gardens, landscape paintings and landscape poems gained popularity among the literati. At the same time, penjing as a form of art with similar themes began to develop.

Zong Bing (375 – 443), a painter of the Northern (439 – 581) and Southern (420 – 589) dynasties, enjoyed roaming from mountain to mountain. When old age and illness prevented him from traveling, he painted what he had seen on the walls in his room. "I savor the essence of nature while being confined to bed to clear my mind to realize the Dao," he said. In *Preface on Landscape Painting*, the first Chinese discussion on landscape painting, he promoted the idea that drawing a landscape painting is a process in which images are created by the painter's

Fresco of Eastern Han Excavated at Wangdu, Hebei Province
The earliest record of a combination of plants, a container, and a frame is in the fresco in the entrance hall of an Eastern Han tomb excavated at Wangdu in Hebei Province: a round pottery tray is placed on a square stand with six red flowers in it. The use of the frame indicates that bonsai was already practiced as an art form in the Eastern Han dynasty.

(facing page)

Yangzhou Garden of Qing Dynasty
Most traditional Chinese gardens feature trees, rocks, water and structures. While trees are carefully pruned, decorative rocks are necessary. The layout is similar to that of water and land penjing. The Yangzhou garden of the Qing dynasty in the painting can be regarded as a super large penjing.

perception of "a short distance away, and yet miles apart" and that "it is the small details that make up the big picture." His theory was a great contribution to the maturity of Chinese landscape painting as well as penjing, an art form that allows one to "savor the essence of nature" at home.

Therefore, penjing is an art form created by the literati for the cultivation of their character, personality, temperament, interests and conceptualization of beauty. At the philosophical level, the artistic value and function of penjing is on par with that of landscape poetry, landscape brush painting or landscape art. These Chinese art forms have been interacting with and growing into each other in a dynamic process.

Early Tang Dynasty

The years of progress and stability during the Tang dynasty (618 – 907) saw quite a number of Chinese art forms, such as poetry, ink painting and sculpture, flourished and matured. The well-known wall mural painting on a corridor leading to the tomb of the Tang Prince Zhang Huai, built in 706, at the Qianling Mausoleum site in Shaanxi Province shows a maidservant carrying a penjing with miniature

rockeries and fruit trees. This indicates that penjing has already begun to develop during the period, with rocks incorporated to create artistic scenery. The arrangement of rocks and trees resemble that of today's tree-in-rock penjing or water and land penjing.

The popularity of penjing in and out of the royal court has been well recorded in paintings and other historical documents from the Tang dynasty; various poets and essayists praised dwarf-potted landscapes. Wang Wei (701? – 761), a poet and painter, "grew orchids in broad-mouthed porcelain jars, and used rocks with beautiful patterns to enhance them." In one of his poems, Tang poet Li He (790 – 816) described the techniques of wiring and pruning he used to care for his pine penjing. His affection for this particular pine encouraged his mind to wander without impediment.

Landscape penjing as an art form had matured in the Tang dynasty as well. One of Yan Liben's (601 – 673) paintings, *Tribute Offered by a Vassal*, depicts a scene of people presenting low-rimmed containers and bizarre rocks as gifts to the court.

The tri-colored glazed pottery ink stone for the grinding and containment of ink, unearthed in a Tang tomb in Zhongbao village in the west suburb of Xi'an city in Shaanxi Province, is in the form of a landscape penjing.

In poems and documents of the Tang dynasty, you can find a lot of descriptions of rockwork, pools, ponds, layouts of stones and man-made hillocks. It was evidence of the popularity of miniature landscapes in people's yards. The larger pieces of work could be a small pool with several pieces of carefully selected rocks, always before the hall or in the yard, while the smaller

ones could be a basin with aquatic plants and animals in it. These were probably early versions of penjing.

In his poem *Rockwork* composed in the year of 742, Du Fu (712 – 770), known as the "saint poet" in Chinese literary history, described the miniature hills that his uncle created in front of his wife's house. In the short preface accompanying the poem, Du Fu marveled about how a couple of baskets of soil could build a hill and how the bamboos planted around the hills shaded them, as if it was another world.

It is evident from these poems that penjing at the time was designed in quite a number of styles using materials such as trees, plants, rock, soil and water.

Rock collecting had become extremely popular during the period, and pieces of unusual quality, patterns and shapes became another theme in the Tang poems. They include, among others, Bai Juyi's (772 – 846) *Taihui Rocks* and *Twin Rocks*, and Li Deyu's (787 – 850) *Bizarre Stone*, *Poem on Luofu Stone*, *Deer-shaped Rock* and *Stalagmite in the Sea*. In addition to his several poems about rocks, Bai Juyi wrote *Essay on Taihu Rocks* in 843, the first Chinese discussion on collecting and appreciation of Taihu rocks, to share his perspective on rock collecting and, in the process, his philosophy of life.

Song and Yuan Dynasties

With ink painting achieving great distinction during the Song dynasty (960 – 1279), so too was penjing poised for dynamic artistic development. It benefited significantly from the landscape and flower-bird paintings of the time, as well as theoretical research into those art forms. As a result, collecting peculiar rocks and appreciating strange trees had grown into a common trend among both the members of the imperial court and common people.

The penjing scene in *Emperor Tang Minghuang Spying on a Bathing Lady*, by Zhang Zeduan, a painter of the Northern Song dynasty (960 – 1127), features an aged pine with fissured bark, elliptic leaves and exposed roots. There is also a penjing scene in the Southern Song painter Liu Songnian's *Eighteen Scholars*. These paintings and poems are evidence that penjing as an art form had been practiced at an advanced artistic level, and tree penjing and landscape penjing, the two main tiers of penjing, had emerged.

Poems from the Song dynasty also show that techniques of producing a landscape penjing at the time were much better, the criteria for rock appreciation were more accurate and researches on rocks achieved new breakthroughs. Mi Fu (1051 – 1107), a great painter obsessed with collecting rocks, suggested that the four essential qualities of an ideal rock were *shou* (an elegant, slender shape), *zhou* (rich surface textures and furrows created from delicate intaglio lines and relief ridges), *lou* (channels and other types of indentations that lend an exquisite beauty to rocks), and *tou* (holes and openness), meaning the best rocks had to be "with a thin and seemingly transparent body, communicative holes and markings." His view made quite an impact on his contemporaries and connoisseurs in the following periods.

The water and land penjing has its beginnings in the Song dynasty. In a *ci* praising a plum in a pond, Lu Shengyi depicts the plum with sparse branches in a pond accompanied by beautifully carved stones and a pagoda, a scene can only be seen at the side of the breathtaking West Lake in Hangzhou, Zhejiang Province.

As the lifestyle of the literati during the Song dynasty was greatly appreciated by Japanese scholars, the craft of penjing was brought to Japan in the late Heian period to the early Kamakura period (1192 – 1333).

Xiezi jing, or tiny scenery, was advocated in the Yuan dynasty (1279 – 1368). The monk Yun Shangren,

Bird Standing on a Rock in Pot, by Emperor Huizong of Song Dynasty
A true artist, Emperor Huizong (1082–1135) is best known for his paintings of birds and flowers. This painting features a bird with a rock and sweet sedge, very pretty and interesting. The rock appears to be Taihu rock.

Emperor Tang Minghuang Spying on a Bathing Lady, by Zhang Zeduan
Zhang Zeduan (1085–1145), a painter in the Northern Song dynasty, is known for his *Scenes along the River During the Qingming Festival*. The penjing in this painting features an aged pine with fissured bark, elliptic leaves and exposed roots.

33

轮囷离奇

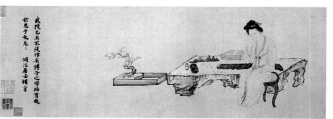

Wu Lingchun, by Wu Wei (1459 – 1508)
This painting features Wu Lingchun, a girl who died of depression because of her failed attempt to free her boyfriend from jail. The Chinese Plum penjing in the painting is a symbol of her nobleness and virtuousness. It has a land part on the left and a water part on the right, indicating the popularity of water and land penjing during the period.

Detail of *Enjoyment in Spring*, by Unknown Painter
This painting features concubines in an imperial palace enjoying themselves on a spring day. The pine penjing in the lower left corner has an aged pine with a curvy trunk beside a bizarre rock and its cloud-shaped foliage progresses towards the right and left sides. This painting, along with Li Shixing's *Dwarf Siberian Pine*, indicates that penjing with both trees and rocks in it was quite popular at the time.

Detail of *Night Revels of Han Xizai*, by Tang Yin (1470 – 1523)
This is a replica by Tang Yin of *Night Revels of Han Xizai*, which was originally composed by the Southern Tang painter Gu Hongzhong (910? – 980?). The tree in the container has a curved trunk with the lateral branches extending out. The exquisite container (and the frame) is probably made of marble.

Dwarf Siberian Pine, by Li Shixing (1282 – 1328)
The aged pine with a curvy trunk and exposed roots portrayed in this Yuan dynasty painting shows little difference in design from penjing specimen we see today in China.

who enjoyed traveling from place to place throughout his life, created penjing to "see the big from the tiny." This practice became an important guiding principle in penjing design in the following centuries. Ding Henian, a Chinese poet of Hui ethnicity in the late Yuan dynasty, said in one of his poems about a penjing created by Yun Shangren; in a pot with trees, rocks and water he imagined the vast Bohai Sea and towering Kongtong Mountains.

The penjing depicted in the Yuan dynasty painting *Dwarf Siberian Pine* shows little difference in design from the penjing specimen we see today in China.

Ming and Qing Dynasties

The Ming dynasty (1368 – 1644) saw the peak of penjing creation. While different styles with matured craftsmanship can be derived from historical documents and archeological relics, efforts were made to theorize about the art by the use of source trees, rock selecting, design, display and appreciation.

Tu Long (1543 – 1605), a writer of the Ming dynasty, declared that "the best penjing are smaller ones that can be set on a stool or table; then come those that can be placed in a courtyard." In addition to his considerations of size and composition of penjing, he stressed the importance of poetic image in the art of penjing. Tu Long suggested that the designs of aged trees in the paintings by Ma Yuan, Guo Xi, Liu Songnian and Sheng Zizhao be followed. To be specific, "a couple of Taiwan pines can be arranged high and low in a pot in the yard, with exquisitely chiseled stalagmite rocks interspersed between them. In front of a single-tree penjing, you feel as if you were wondering under a single pine on a hill, while a forest penjing makes you feel as if you were in a forest, where you forget about the heat in a hot July day." At the same time, "hemp or palm stem fibers can be used to wire the branches to design the style, but no trace of such artificial efforts should be left after the removal of the fibers, as if it were totally created by nature."

Similar introductions to the design and appreciation of penjing art can be found in essays by Zeng Mianzhi, Wang Mingshao, Wang Xiangjin, Wen Zhenheng, Qu Dajun, Lu Yancan, Wu Chutai and Lin Youlin.

In the Qing dynasty (1644 – 1911) , penjing art became more varied in design and in style, more source materials were used and better containers were produced.

The observation by Liu Luan (c. 1240 – 1324) of the penjing in the early Qing dynasty exhibited trees, rocks, soil, water and fish: "Tree penjing and landscape penjing are created for pleasure. Tree branches are shortened by wiring and pruning, and large rocks are cut. Some trees are only a few inches tall but bear fruits, some containers are several feet long and contain fish. These creations are called penjing. In Yuan dynasty, people referred to them as *xiezi jing*, or tiny scenery." What he described is now known as "water and land penjing."

Due to its improvement in cultivating and designing techniques, more diverse forms and styles and increasing regional popularity, penjing art reached unprecedented heights during the reigns of Emperors Kangxi (1662 – 1722) and Jiaqing (1796 – 1820). At the same time, the number of publications about the art increased dramatically, among which *Designing Penjing* by Chen Haozi and *On Penjing* by Su Ling are believed to be the most detailed and influential.

In his *On Penjing*, Su Ling metaphorically classified

penjing source plants into four sages, seven maters, eighteen scholars and four elegant flowers. Chen Haozi devoted a whole chapter of his *Designing Penjing* to the selection of trees and plants for penjing. He also explained how to grow lichens or mosses to decorate penjing: "Lichens and mosses can be added to decorate penjing with flowers and rocks. To grow them, a mixture of pond sludge and horse manure is often applied to areas or tree forks with proper moisture."

In *Penjing in Yangzhou*, Li Dou said that during the reign of Emperor Qianlong, penjing that contained flowers and trees, or water and soil, even waterfall, had already appeared in Yangzhou. Due to the popularity of classical gardens and penjing at that time, "nearly every family in Yangzhou plant flowers and have penjing in their houses." He also mentioned in this book that the penjing designed by a monk named Lihuan in Suzhou was always sold at a very high price due to his excellent techniques and unique design.

Various scenes of penjing in paintings by Zheng Banqiao and Huang Shen show how popular penjing was at the time especially in the regions south of the Yangtze River. Penjing art benefited directly from the vigorous artistic development of landscape garden during the Qing dynasty, and many penjing, especially water and land penjing, followed the techniques used in garden art. *The Mustard Seed Garden Painting Manual*, the

Tianning Temple Pine
Species: *Juniperus formosana* (Taiwan Juniper)
Age of tree: Over 400 years old
Height of tree: 66 cm
Container: Rectangular stone tray
Introduction: This is a penjing pine from Tianning Temple from the late Ming dynasty in Yangzhou, China. Two-thirds of the twisted dragon-shaped trunk is dead. The cloud-shape foliage is among the popular styles of tree penjing in the area.

A Porcelain Pot of Qing Dynasty Produced in Jingdezhen, Jiangxi Province
Porcelain containers produced in Jingdezhen often features traditional landscape painting and flower-bird painting. This pot of Qing dynasty is collected at Penjing Museum of Yangzhou.

A Sandy Clay Pot of Qing Dynasty Produced in Yixing, Jiangsu Province
The rustic and earthy containers produced in Yixing are perfect foils for trees and plants due to its air permeability. This pot of Qing dynasty is collected at Penjing Museum of Yangzhou.

A Glazed Pottery Pot of Qing Dynasty Produced in Shiwan, Guangdong Province
Containers produced in Shiwan are known for their bright colors and regional features. This pot of Qing dynasty is a private collection.

Detail of *The Emperor Qianlong's Southern Inspection Tour* (Scroll Six), by Xu Yang
A native of Suzhou and court painter, Xu Yang was commissioned by the Emperor Qianlong (1736 – 1795) to record in twelve monumental handscrolls the emperor's historic tour in southern China. The painting was created during the period from 1764 to 1769. In this painting was a scene of Suzhou, in which penjing specimens are found in a yard and on boats in the river before the houses. It looks like a penjing market.

Chinese Plum Penjing, by Wang Tubing (1668 – 1743) of Qing Dynasty
The plum in the painting has two echoing trunks, with one dominating the design, in a fine Chinese-crabapple-shaped glazed pottery pot.

first published manual for Chinese painting, became a popular reference for penjing enthusiasts. At this stage, Chinese penjing became a well-established art which pursued images of poetry and painting.

The development of the pottery industry in the Ming and Qing dynasties offered various styles of quality containers. Porcelain pots from Jingdezhen in Jiangxi Province, sandy clay and glazed pottery from Yixing in Jiangsu Province and glazed containers from Shiwan in Guangdong Province were greatly valued for more aesthetically refined penjing specimens.

The Seventh Chinese National Penjing Convention and Exhibition (2008)
The exhibition was held at Xuanwuhu, Nanjing, from September 29 to October 6, 2008. Sponsored by the Chinese Society of Landscape Architecture, Department of Construction of Jiangsu Province, and People's Government of Nanjing Municipality, it attracted nearly 1,000 specimens by artists from 108 cities, including Hong Kong, Macao, and Taiwan. The specimens were grouped into four categories: tree penjing, landscape penjing, water and land penjing, and miniature penjing. It was the most influential national penjing exhibition ever held in China.

Recent Renaissance

Chinese penjing art experienced a decline since the end of the Qing dynasty before its renaissance in the late 1970s, when penjing gardens were built in many regions in China, ancient penjing specimens were discovered, new penjing designs were created and exhibitions were held. The turning point was the Penjing Art Exhibition held in Beijing from September 11 to October 24, 1979.

The Chinese Association of Flower and Penjing was established on December 4, 1981 and was later re-organized as the Flower, Penjing and Stone Branch under the larger Chinese Society of Landscape Architecture. The association holds a penjing exhibition every four years and so far it has successfully held seven times from 1985 to 2008 in Shanghai, Wuhan, Tianjin, Yangzhou, Suzhou, Quanzhou and Nanjing.

The establishment of the Chinese Penjing Artists Association in 1988 has encouraged more exhibitions and training projects in many places in China, thus increase the popularity of penjing art and the number of penjing connoisseurs.

As a result, the art form has been gaining popularity and more local clubs have been formed for designers to display their specimens and to share their techniques. Penjing gardens have been built in many cities in China

China (Chencun) International Bonsai and Suiseki Exhibition (2006)
The exhibition was held at in Chencun, Guangdong Province from April 30 to May 7, 2006. Sponsored by the Chinese Society of Landscape Architecture, Bonsai Clubs International, and People's Government of Shunde District, it attracted more than 600 penjing and stone specimens by artists from all over the world. Fifteen lectures and performances involving 20 artists were conducted. It was the first international penjing and stone exhibition held in Mainland China.

and more specimens have been exported to a number of countries and regions.

With advances in technique and new means of communication, publications on the theoretical aspects of the art have increased significantly in the past years.

Changes in people's lifestyles and aesthetic tastes have also led to experiments with innovative forms and techniques. The process has been greatly aided by discoveries of new species and rock categories. As a result, more unique and creative specimens are designed.

In the past thirty years, Chinese penjing artists have been active in exhibitions held in more than ten countries and regions in Europe, Asia and America, as well as Hong Kong and Macau. They have been invited to international penjing conferences for the purpose of demonstrations. Several international events were also successfully held in China, including the 4th APBSCE (Asia-Pacific Bonsai and Suiseki Convention and Exhibition) in Shanghai in October 1997 and 10th APBSCE in Beijing in September 2005 and China (Chencun) International Bonsai and Suiseki Exhibition (2006), which was hosted by the Chinese Society of Landscape Architecture, Bonsai Clubs International and the People's Government of Shunde District. These events have been great opportunities for penjing and bonsai artists from different cultural backgrounds to meet.

In 2013, the convention of Bonsai Clubs International and the exhibition of World Bonsai Friendship Federation will be held in Yangzhou and Changzhou, respectively, providing forums for Chinese penjing artists to showcase their talents.

CHAPTER THREE
BASIC PENJING TECHNIQUES

Penjing has borrowed heavily from formative art, garden art, and hand crafted art. This chapter serves as an introduction to tools used in penjing creation, characteristics of various categories of species, rock, soil, container and miniature, the basics in propagating, maintaining and caring for penjing plants, and techniques to process trees and rocks in penjing design.

It has to be noted that penjing as a practical art can never be learned from books alone. Any success is the result of repeated practice and accumulation of related knowledge.

Penjing Tools

Tools needed to create and maintain penjing specimens consist of the following categories.

(Re)potting Tools
A **soil sieve set** with different sized meshes that allow you to create uniformity by removing large particles in soil.

A **root hook** is used to remove old soil on the roots and to untangle them during repotting.

Plastic meshes are for covering the drainage holes of penjing containers.

A **soil scoop set** is used to place soil exactly where you need it.

A **bamboo rod** is used to tamp soil

into pot and around roots. It can also be used to remove old roots or to untangle them.

A **penjing brush** is used to clean the outside of pots or worktables.

Shaping Tools
Standard penjing shears are commonly used to prune away medium or small sized branches.

The **concave branch cutter** is used to remove large branches. It is available in three sizes: small, medium and large.

Long handled bud shears are for the finest details and precision cuts. They are available in two sizes: small and large.

Garden shears are used for general purposes in garden art, but mainly for pruning large branches or roots in penjing.

A **knob cutter** is designed to remove trunk knobs and roots.

Metal wire allows penjing artists to better control and manipulate the trunks and branches of their penjing to shape them into the desired structure. While aluminum wire is used, annealed copper wire is better as it retains its holding power once applied to your tree and will not damage branches. Wire of various sizes is needed for different branches.

A **wire cutter** is designed specifically for cutting metal wire. It is available in various shapes.

Wire pliers are used to coil wire around the limbs of the penjing or to remove it.

A **garden saw** is very useful when cutting large branches or roots that are too big for branch cutters.

Gravers are designed for the removal of the barks of tree trunks or branches in the style known as *sheli* penjing, or *shari* in Japanese bonsai. They can be sickle-, half-circle- or angled-razor-shaped.

An **engraving machine** is also designed for use of *sheli* style.

A **grafting knife** is used for grafting and cutting branches.

A **turntable** is very handy for getting all the way around the penjing when training, maintaining, and trimming. They can be on a table or on a stand.

Cutting and Polishing Tools
A **chisel** is designed to create markings or holes on rocks. It is also used for chiseling tree trunks.

Hammers are often used in the design of landscape penjing. Popular hand-powered variations include pointed hammer, ball-peen, and framing hammer.

(facing page)

Gorgeous Flowers
Species: *Rhododendron simsii* (Azalea)
Age of tree: 40 years old
Height of tree: 46 cm
Container: Oval sandy clay tray
Designer: Zhao Qingquan
Introduction: Azalea is a popular penjing species for its gorgeous flowers. This specimen has been trained from a tree with several trunks. The unwanted trunks were removed, leaving one trunk and its stunning roots, to fully display its beauty.

A **rock cutter** is designed to cut hard rocks.

A **copper brush** is used to clean and polish chiseled rock surfaces to make them as smooth as possible.

A **scraper** is used to remove residues when cementing pieces of rocks.

An **oil painting brush** is used to remove the residue between rocks joined together with cement.

Maintenance Tools

A **watering can** with its long neck is designed specifically for watering and fertilizing penjing plants.

A **sprayer** is for disbursing small drops of chemicals used in penjing maintenance and care. It is sometimes used to spray water on the leaves of a tree. It is usually available in two sizes.

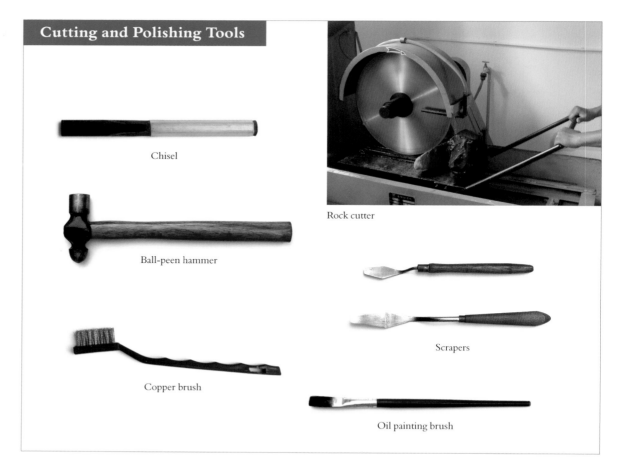

Cutting and Polishing Tools

Chisel

Ball-peen hammer

Rock cutter

Scrapers

Copper brush

Oil painting brush

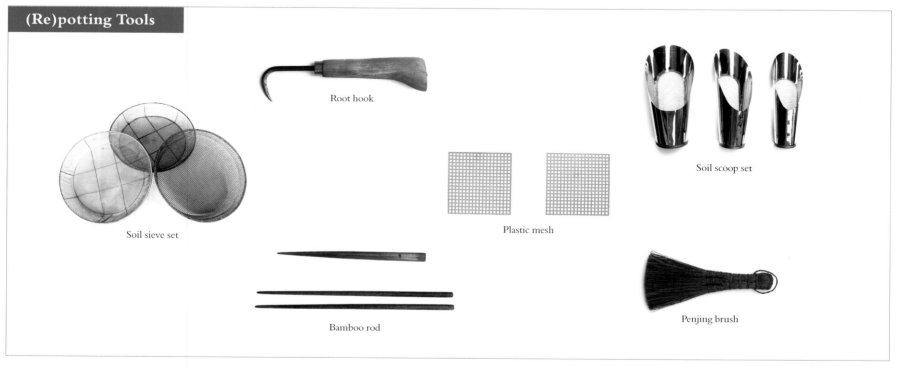

(Re)potting Tools

Root hook

Soil scoop set

Soil sieve set

Plastic mesh

Bamboo rod

Penjing brush

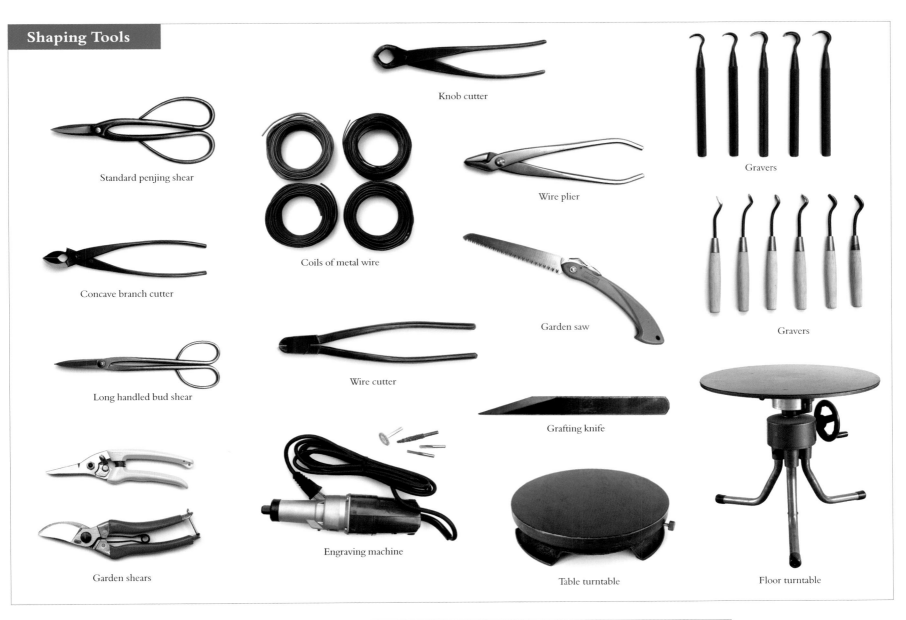

Shaping Tools

Standard penjing shear

Concave branch cutter

Long handled bud shear

Garden shears

Knob cutter

Coils of metal wire

Wire cutter

Engraving machine

Wire plier

Garden saw

Grafting knife

Table turntable

Gravers

Gravers

Floor turntable

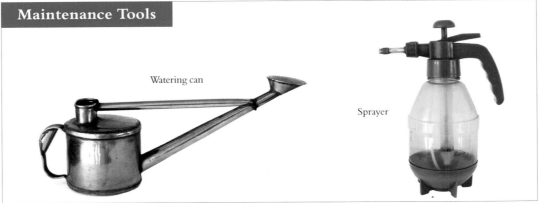

Maintenance Tools

Watering can

Sprayer

41

Soil

A penjing is confined to a relatively small space and needs the necessities of water, air, and nutrients. Therefore, the soil in which the tree and/or other plants grow is an essential item for its good health. Many a penjing become sick or even die due to problems with the soil.

While it is through the soil that plants are able to obtain water and nutrients to grow, the soil is also part of the design because it serves as the landscape.

Many factors contribute to a good soil mix:

Good water-retention. The soil needs to be able to hold and retain sufficient quantities of water and nutrients to supply moisture and nutrition to the penjing.

Good drainage. Excess water must be able to drain immediately from the pot. Soil lacking good drainage is too water retentive, lack aeration, and is liable to a build-up of salts, which can result in root rot. For a good soil structure that drains well, soils are often sifted to remove dust and very small particles.

Good aeration. The particles used in a penjing mix should allow tiny gaps or air pockets between each particle. It is important to the health of the roots that they have access to oxygen, and it also creates favorable conditions for the growth of the bacteria which is needed to decompose fertilizers so the plants can absorb the nutrients.

Proper pH value. Different species vary in their requirements for the chemical properties of the soil. Some prefer the soil that is slightly acid, while some need the soil that is slightly alkaline. Therefore, the soil has to be carefully selected according to the biological properties of different species. As a rule, the pH value should be between 6 and 7.5.

Soil mixes can be organic or inorganic. Dead plant matters such as peat, humus, or pine bark are described as being organic soil components, which contain rich nutrients but can be too water retentive. Inorganic soil mixes contain little or no organic matter; instead, they are made up of specially formulated soils such as silica sand, weathered granite, calcined (baked), or fired clays. The advantage of inorganic materials is that they hold their open structure for a long time without breaking down into mush. Pines and junipers, for instance, require less water than most other species, so they prefer inorganic soil mixes, while broad-leaved tree species require more water and are usually planted in organic soil mixes. There is no single soil mix that is best for cultivating penjing; variables such as local soil types, local climate, and individual tree species all contribute to variations in one's soil mixes.

A sieve set with three different sized meshes is suggested for the preparation of the soil of your penjing. The large mesh removes the largest particles, the medium mesh grades the soil, and the small mesh is used to remove the dust afterwards.

Source Trees

The tree is often the dominant element in the composition of a penjing, and generally trees with twisted and coiled roots, a dense or pleasing foliage, or striking flowers or fruits are selected to be penjing trees. Other considerations include biological features such as sprouting ability, response to pruning, and life span.

Tree Sources

Trees for penjing can be tree stumps, and they can also be propagated.

Tree stumps can be dug out and trained to grow as penjing trees. When selecting a stump, the type of tree species, its age and shape, and its prospects for growth should be taken into consideration. The best choices are usually fancy, mature trees with strong and curvy trunks or branches and agreeable roots.

Peat.

Pine bark.

Silica sand.

The best time to dig a tree stump out is when it is in the state of dormancy before it begins to develop in the early spring.

When a tree is being uprooted, the lateral roots and fibrous roots are kept while the taproot is often cut off (see top picture). In keeping with its shape and future growth, when it is pruned again only a few primary branches are kept but considerably shortened. However, more branches should be left for pines, junipers, and other evergreen trees due to their lack of sprouting ability. Stumps that have been dug out should be replanted as soon as possible.

Penjing source trees can also be propagated from seeds, cuttings, layering, grafting, or plant division. By any of these processes, it takes the grower about three to five years before a tree can be potted, which is why artists often buy their source trees from nursery gardens instead.

Training Process

It takes about a year for a stump to grow into a tree to be potted and designed.

During the process, the stump can be trained and regularly cared for in another container (see middle picture) or any other fertile soil with good drainage and sunlight (see bottom picture).

Stumps are usually planted in deep soil, with bud eyes above the surface of the soil. Mosses or lichens are often used to cover higher stumps to keep the loss of moisture at a minimum. A thorough soaking is needed after a stump is planted. Shading measures are needed in the summer, while straw mats can be used to protect it from the cold during the winter. It should be watered regularly, especially when it is in its period of fast growth; however, over watering results in root rot. When it is dry, water can be sprayed on the leaves. While fertilizing is important for all stumps, newly planted ones need to be fed with small dosages frequently. Diluted cake fertilizers that have been thoroughly decomposed are often used.

Pruning, wiring, pinching, and taking measures against pests and diseases are necessary before stumps are potted. The pruning work comprise of the regular and timely removal of dead and sick branches, as well as branches that do not contribute to the desired penjing shape. Wiring allows artists to control and manipulate the trunk and branches before they become difficult to shape into position. All these jobs need to be done by following the general guidelines of penjing art, with the features of your particular stump in your mind.

A tree stump being pruned.

Right Species

A variety of species can be chosen as penjing trees, but typically, trees with dense or pleasing foliage or with striking flowers or fruits are ideal. Other considerations include biological features such as sprouting ability, response to pruning, and lifespan. Up to now, about 200 species have been trained for the purpose of penjing, which largely fall into two categories: coniferous and deciduous trees.

The following is a list of the common types of trees that are trained for use as penjing specimens, but it is far from being exhaustive as China is very rich in source trees and new species are being used all the time.

A tree stump trained in a pot for its shape.

Tree stumps trained outdoors in loose, fertile land with good drainage and adequate sunlight.

Soughing of Wind in Pines
Species: *Pinus parviflora* (Japanese Five Needle Pine)
Age of (main) tree: 30 years old
Type of rock: Ying Rock
Container: Oval marble tray
Length of container: 100 cm
Designer: Zhao Qingquan
Introduction: This is a water and land penjing with a sparse forest, with a clear sense of dominance and subordination, emptiness and substance, denseness and sparseness, and straightness and curviness. The old man (miniature) is sitting under the trees, as if enjoying the sound of wind in pines or the sound of the waves from the sea.

Charm of the Orient
Species: *Juniperus formosana* (Taiwan Juniper)
Age of tree: 80 years old
Height of tree: 84 cm
Container: Rectangular sandy clay tray
Designer: Wang Xin
Introduction: This is a huge Taiwan Juniper with a natural beautiful shape. The *sheli* indicates the age of the tree, while the green foliage shows how vigorous it is.

Coniferous Species. Coniferous species refers to evergreen pines, junipers, and cedars. These species are preferred by penjing artists for their features; large size, firmness, vigor, roughness, and unchanging color during the year, to show their "inner spirit."

Picea asperata Dragon Spruce
Pinus parviflora Japanese Five Needle Pine
Pinus bungeana Lacebark Pine
Pinus taiwanensis Taiwan Pine
Pinus thunbergii Japanese Black Pine
Pinus thunbergii var. corticosa Japanese Cork-bark Black Pine
Pinus densiflora Japanese Red Pine
Pinus tabulaeformis Chinese Hard Pine
Pseudolarix amabilis Golden Larch
Podocarpus macrophyllus Buddhist Pine
Podocarpus macrophyllus var. maki Yew Plum Pine
Juniperus chinensis Chinese Juniper
Juniperus chinensis var. Sargentii Sargent's Juniper
Sabina chinensis cv. kaizuka Dragon Juniper
Juniperus formosana Taiwan Juniper
Juniperus rigida Needle Juniper

Platycladus orientalis Chinese Arborvitae
Cupressus funebris Chinese Weeping Cypress
Sabina procumbens Procumbent Juniper
Metasequoia glyptostroboides Dawn Redwood
Cryptomeria japonica Japanese Cedar
Taxodium distichum Common Baldcypress
Glyptostrobus pensilis Chinese Swamp Cypress
Taxus cuspidata var. umbraculifera Low Japanese Yew

Deciduous Species. Deciduous species refers to trees other than coniferous species, mainly including broad-leaved trees which can be grown as penjing specimens for their shapes, leaves, flowers, fruits, and vines. These trees are often trained to feature their feminine natures—gentleness, delicacy, elegance, gracefulness and variety of color.

The Depth of Shade
Species: *Ulmus parvifolia* (Chinese Elm)
Age of (main) tree: 60 years old
Type of rock: Turtle Shell Rock
Container: Rectangular marble tray
Length of container: 120 cm
Designer: Meng Guangling
Introduction: The Chinese Elm trees and the Turtle Shell Rock feature a country landscape, with the help of the land mass covered with mosses and grasses. The main tree is straight and upright, but with horizontal branches, while the other smaller trees contrast with it in terms of their various movements. The shoreline is geologically varied but natural looking.

The Spirit of Li Bai
Species: *Buxus sinica* (Chinese Box)
Age of tree: 90 years old
Height of tree: 80 cm
Container: Rectangular sandy clay tray
Designer: Xu Ronglin
Introduction: This literati style penjing portrays the natural and unrestrained character of Li Bai (701–762), a Tang dynasty poet known for his glorification of alcoholic beverages. The specimen is graceful but with tension and flaunty but with restraint.

Shape-Effect Plants

Ulmus parvifolia Chinese Elm
Sageretia theezans Chinese Bird Plum
Zelkova serrata Japanese Zelkova
Celtis sinensis Chinese Hackberry
Buxus sinica Chinese Box
Buxus harlandii Harlands Box
Murraya paniculata Orange Jasmine
Poilaniella fragilis Polan
Tamarix chinensis Chinese Tamarisk
Carpinus turczaninowii Korean Hornbeam
Ligustrum quihoui Purpus Privet
Vitex negundo Chinese Chastetree
Ficus microcarpa Chinese Banyan
Carmona microphylla Fukien Tea
Fraxinus chinensis Chinese Ash
Xylosma japonicum Shiny Xylosma
Syzrgium buxifolium Myrtaceae

Foliage Plants

Acer palmatum Japanese Maple
Acer buergerianum Trident Maple
Ginkgo biloba Maidenhair Tree
Euonymus alatus Burning Bush
Bambusoideae Bamboo
Bambusa multiplex cv. Fernleaf Fernleaf
    Hedge Bamboo

(below)

Night in the Country
Species: *Bambusa multiplex cv. fernleaf* (Fernleaf Hedge Bamboo)
Type of rock: Ying Rock
Length of container: 60 cm
Container: Rectangular marble tray
Designer: Jiang Hongliu
Introduction: The bamboos, the bridge and the pavilion make a perfect yard. With bamboos as the main component and accompanying rocks, the design features the techniques used in Chinese gardens, where bamboos often dominate a landscape to smybolize the virtues and integrity of the literati.

(above left)

The Color of Autumn
Species: *Acer palmatum* (Japanese Maple)
Age of (main) tree: 6 years old
Type of rock: Ying Rock
Container: Oval marble tray
Length of container: 70 cm
Designer: Chen Yougui
Introduction: With several small Japanese Maple trees, this water and land landscape shows variation in both height and movements of the trees. The sharp contrast between the red leaves and dark rocks enhances the sense of autumn in the landscape.

(above right)

Frost and Red Leaves in Autumn
Species: *Acer buergerianum* (Trident Maple)
Age of tree: 40 years old
Height of tree: 85 cm
Container: Rectangular glazed pottery tray
Designer: Zheng Yongtai
Introduction: The Trident Maple, a typical foliage-effect penjing tree, is loved for its red leaves in autumn especially after being frosted. The sharp contrast between the movements of the trunk of the tree and its branches contributes greatly to the variation and balance of the composition.

Flower-Effect Plants

Prunus mume Chinese Plum
Chimonanthus praecox Wintersweet
Lagerstroe indica Crape Myrtle
Malus spectabilis Chinese Flowering Crabapple
Malus halliana Hall Crabapple
Malus micromalus Midget Crabapple
Rhododendron simsii Azalea
Chaenomeles speciosa Chinese Quince
Camellia sasanqua Christmas Camellia
Camellia japonica Japanese Camellia
Elaeocarpus sylvestris Elaeocarpus
Serissa foetita Snowrose
Osmanthus fragrans Sweet Osmanthus
Loropetalum chinense var. rubrum   Chinese
   Fringe Flower
Cercis chinensis Chinese Redbud
Prunus persica Peach
Bougainvillea spectabilis Brazil Bougainvillea
Jasminum nudiflorum Winter Jasmine
Caragana sinica Chinese Peashrub
Gardenia jasminoides Cape Jasmine

Sword and Flowers
Species: *Loropetalum chinense var. rubrum* (Chinese Fringe Flower)
Age of tree: 60 years old
Height of tree: 125 cm
Container: Chinese-crabapple-shaped sandy clay pot
Designer: Zheng Yongtai
Introduction: Chinese Fringe Flower is trained for its gorgeous flowers in spring as well as its ornamental red leaves when it is without flowers. This specimen has been trained from an earlier stump. The dead trunk is just like a long sword pointing to the sky, in sharp contrast with the living tree and the striking color of the flowers.

(above left)

Golden Autumn
Species: *Diospyros armata* (Spiny Persimmon)
Age of tree: 80 years old
Height of tree: 58 cm
Container: Rectangular glazed pottery tray
Designer: Zhao Qingquan
Introduction: Spiny Persimmon is known for the stunning contrast between its golden berries and green leaves and dark branches in autumn. Trained from a stump, the persimmon in the container has the long exposed roots as its trunks.

(above right)

Brilliance in Autumn
Species: *Pyracantha fortuneana* (Chinese Firethorn)
Age of tree: 30 years old
Height of tree: 65 cm
Container: Oval sandy clay tray
Designer: Zhao Qingquan
Introduction: Chinese Firethorn as a popular penjing species produces bright-colored small berries. With a curry trunk and sparse but well-spaced foliage, this firethorn resembles a literati penjing.

Fruit-Effect Plants

Punica granatum Pomegranate
Crataegus pinnatifida Chinese Hawthorn
Ilex cornuta Chinese Holly
Damnacanthus indicus Indian Damnacanthus
Diospyros armata Spiny Persimmon
Diospyros rthombifolia Princess Persimmon
Pyracantha fortuneana Chinese Firethorn
Elaeagnus pungens Silverthorn
Berberis thunbergii Japanese Barberry
Chaenomeles sinensis Chinese Flowering
    Quince
Malus pumila Common Apple
Malus prunifolia Chinese Apple

Diospyros Kaki Japanese Persimmon
Cotoneaster horizontalis Rock Cotoneaster
Stranvaesia davidiana Chinese Stranvaesia

Vines

Lonicera japonica Japanese Honeysuckle
Trachelospermum jasminoides Chinese
    Starjasmine
Hedera nepalensis Nepal Ivy
Parthenocissus tricuspidata Japanese Creeper
Campsis grandiflora Chinese Trumpet Vine
Wisteria sinensis Chinese Wisteria
Wisteria Floribunda Japanese Wisteria
Euonymus fortunei Winter Creeper

Golden and Silver Flowers
Species: *Lonicera japonica* (Japanese Honeysuckle)
Age of tree: 30 years old
Height of tree: 85 cm
Container: Rectangular sandy clay tray
Designer: Wang Xin
Introduction: Japanese Honeysuckle is a climbing vine trained for its shape as well as its creamy to yellow fragrant flowers. This specimen has been pruned into the shape of a tree. When it blooms, golden and silver flowers will cover the whole tree.

Fig. 1 Plastic mesh is used to cover the drainage holes, to stop soil medium from falling through the holes while still allowing the free drainage that is required.

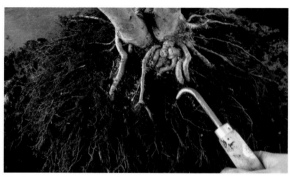

Fig. 2 Untangling roots with a root hook.

Fig. 3 Working soil around the root mass with bamboo rods carefully so that there are no air pockets.

Fig. 4 Larger trees are arranged first for a forest penjing.

Fig. 5 Smaller trees are added.

Fig. 6 Soil is being added when trees are in place.

Fig. 7 Continue to add soil while working it around the root mass with bamboo rods or hand until the root has been covered up with soil.

Fig. 8 Trees can be positioned with wire for desired locations and movements.

Fig. 9 The finished composition.

Fig. 10 Spraying adequate water.

(facing page)

Flying Sheets of Cloud
Species: *Juniperus chinensis var.sargentii* (Sargent's Chinese Juniper)
Age of (main) tree: 25 years old
Height of tree: 85 cm
Container: Oval sandy clay tray
Length of container: 120 cm
Designer: Zhao Qingquan
Introduction: The same penjing two years later. While this juniper penjing is two years old and needs more training, the layout of the trees shows a forest of junipers. The wire used to position the trees has been removed.

Potting

When the pot and soil are prepared, cover the drainage hole of the pot with a plastic mesh, which stops the soil medium from falling through the holes but still allows water to drain (fig. 1). Prune the root mass again according to the location where the tree is to be positioned (fig. 2).

If the pot is shallow, the tree should be held in place with a wire threading through the drainage hole so that it is unable to be rocked by the wind during the weeks when its new roots are growing. When a forest penjing is potted, make sure the trees are positioned according to your design.

Before the tree is positioned in the container, cover the base of the pot with a layer of soil with larger particles and then another layer of finer soil. Place the tree in the pot and then add some soil and work it around the root mass with a bamboo rod carefully so that there are no air pockets (fig. 3). Make sure that the soil is not compressed to allow air and water to penetrate into it. Continue to add soil until the pot is filled just below the rim. The desired shape of the tree decides its depth in the pot, but normally the top of the root is kept near or above the surface of the soil.

Potting forest penjing trees requires more effort than a single tree (figures 4–10).

Usually, pruning is needed after the trees have been placed in position. This is followed by placing a layer of fine "decorative soil", on which small grasses and mosses are often added. When the soil is fully worked in, water the trees thoroughly to ensure that the soil is fully wet. It is important that the newly potted trees are placed in a partially sheltered location without wind and that the compost is kept moist to promote the growth of new roots, before they are cared for and maintained in the normal way.

Fig. 1 Detail of a pruned broad-leaved tree. This is a detail of the penjing entitled *Vigor* (see page 76 for details).

Fig. 2 Parallel branches.

Fig. 3 One of the parallel branches is often removed.

Fig. 4 Crossing branches.

Fig. 5 One of the crossing branches is often removed.

Pruning

Penjing trees are pruned to keep their pleasing shapes by removing or cutting back their branches. Most broad-leaved species are pruned so that they grow better, look more natural, and have better structures (fig.1).

Parallel, crossing, overlapping, symmetrical, and whorled branches are often removed or cut short to keep trees in shape. Some of them have to be wired to benefit the whole structure (figures 2–11).

When a long branch to be pruned is thick enough, cut it back to a pair of lateral branches. Wait until the lateral branches are large enough to be trimmed, and cut them back following the same principle.

Repeated processes like this will result in your desired structure. It is important that only one pair of branches is kept in each pruning and that it is in a fork-shape with one longer than the other. Of course, in some cases a branch may be cut back to only one sub-branch, to thin the foliage mass or avoid crossing branches (figures 12–16).

When several trees are planted in a pot, lower branches are often removed to make the grouping look more natural. Some primary branches in a group of trees may even be cut off because they overlap or cross other branches in the group. Of course, some large branches in a single-tree penjing may also be unnecessary

according to the design and should be removed.

In addition, the roots of penjing trees need pruning as well before they are potted, mainly because the size of the penjing pot only allows a shallow root system. A certain amount of old soil needs to be removed before larger taproots and long twisting roots are cut back. The amount of old soil and the number of roots to be removed depend on the shape and size of the pot. Therefore, when a tree has to be root pruned before it is put into its chosen pot, the root mass has to be removed as little as possible. A second pruning can be done when there is another pot ready to hold it.

52

Fig. 6 Overlapping branches.

Fig. 8 Symmetrical branches.

Fig. 10 Whorled branches.

Fig. 7 One of the overlapping branches is often removed.

Fig. 9 One of the symmetrical branches is often cut off.

Fig. 11 One of the whorled branches is left.

Fig. 12 Branches to be pruned (primary branches).

Fig. 13 A pair of branches kept (first underbranches).

Fig. 15 Pruned for a second time with a pair of underbranches left (second underbranches).

Fig. 14 Well-grown first underbranches.

Fig. 16 Pruned for a third time with a pair of underbranches left (third underbranches).

Fig. 1 Wiring a Japanese Five Needle Pine.

Fig. 2 The wire is applied at a 45° to the direction of the branch that is to be wired.

Fig. 3 The outside of a curve, where the branch bends, is held with the wire.

Wiring

Wiring is an important part of the process of styling your penjing. By coiling wire around the limbs of the tree, the designer is able to manipulate its movement or curve it into a desired position. The technique is used more for pines and junipers than for other species (fig. 1).

Penjing metal wire is often available as aluminum or copper. The actual size of the wire needed will vary according to the strength and thickness of the branches you are wiring. Copper wire can be annealed over heat at a dull red glow, so it bends easily after cooling down. This makes it easier to apply and to allow it to resume its holding power once it is applied to your tree. However, the work done should not be redone as wiring requires a skillful designer. Aluminum wire, pliable and stable, is generally easier to work with for beginners.

Before a tree is wired, allow the pot to dry out slightly before it is re-watered. With less water, the tree will be more pliable and easy to be bent. For more delicate species, hemp fiber or paper can be applied before branches are wired to protect their relatively thin and vulnerable bark.

Wiring should be applied first to the primary branches or branches at a lower level. Where possible, the wire should be applied at 45 degrees angle to the direction of the branch that is to be wired (fig. 2). As you coil the wire further down the branch, push and bend the branch with your thumb. Bend branches slowly and steadily so you can watch for signs of cracking and splitting. The outside of a curve, where the branch bends, should be held with the wire (fig. 3).

It is advisable that the start of the coil is anchored into the soil when wiring the trunk of a tree (fig. 4). The first turn of the wire on the trunk should be secured before you continue; and the last should be reversal to the direction of the branch to secure the end of the wire at the tip.

Fig. 4 When wiring the trunk of a tree, the start of the coil is anchored into the soil in the pot.

Fig. 5 A neighboring branch is involved to secure your control over the branches.

Fig. 6 Wrap larger branches with a piece of hemp fiber before wiring them. A couple of wires can be used along the outside of the branch where it is most likely to split.

Fig. 7 Choose every other sub-branches on a primary branch, when they are to be wired.

Fig. 8 When a second wire is needed to be coiled along the same branch for more support, it must be alone in a parallel manner and avoid crossing the first one.

Fig. 9 Removing wire using a wire cutter.

Neighboring branches can also be involved to secure your control over the branches (fig. 5).

Create movement, either from left to right or from right to left, according to the direction of your intended bend. The movement sometimes is changed by the developments of neighboring branches. The wire should be cut cleanly to avoid sharp ends. A gap of the length of a sewing needle needs to be kept between the wire and the bark of the tree; wire that is coiled too closely damages the branches.

Before wiring the trunk or primary branches, wrap them with pieces of hemp fiber, tape, or cloth to secure the positions of the outer protective layer, the layer of wood of the trunk or branches, and of course, to protect the bark. Two or three wires can be used on the outside of the branch where it is most likely to split before you continue your work of coiling the wire (fig. 6).

Choose every other sub-branch on a primary branch, when they are to be wired (fig. 7). Make sure that at least one turn around the primary branch is done to secure the control of the sub-branches. The end of the wire should be fixed at the back of an internode with the last turn on the primary branch to avoid splitting.

When more than two wires have to be coiled along the same branch, do it in a parallel and neat manner because crossing wires would look messy, and the inner wire may damage the bark (fig. 8).

The length of time you leave a wire on varies depending on the type of tree and its growth rate. Keep a close eye on the wire, and when it starts to look too tight, cut it off. Wire marks are considered ugly and should be avoided by removing the wire before it has a chance to dig into the bark. Great care must be taken when removing the wire. It is recommended that wire cutters be used, because any kind of force to unwind the wire can easily lead to broken branches (fig. 9).

Sheli

An aged tree or a part of a tree that may die, with its wood free of bark or weathered by extreme conditions such as snow, wind, thunder, and lightning or from pests and diseases. These trunks or branches are called *sheli* in Chinese penjing, or *shari* in Japanese bonsai (fig. 1).

Sheli can be created by chiseling or removing a part of the bark of the trunk or branch of a tree. The unusual combination of dead areas contrasting with small signs of life is artistically compelling. *Sheli* is often carved into arresting shapes in trees such as pines and junipers, whose firm wood do not decompose easily.

Usually, a *sheli* penjing has a stretch of *sheli*, or dead wood, running in a zigzag manner in the front of the wood, but accompanied with living veins.

As the living veins move water and nutrients between the roots and branches located higher in the tree, their movements decide the future shape of the tree. Before you start removing the bark, draw the desired shape of the living part on the trunk with chalk. Then proceed with removing the bark with a sharp scalpel. It is important that all the edges of the veins are cut clean and straight, which helps the tree in healing. You may want to start with a narrow strip of bark, which you can widen in stages.

When the whole bark of a branch needs to be removed, take away the leaves first. Remove the bark with a scalpel and pliers. This is followed with the process of carving it into natural-looking dead wood.

Carving should be conducted by tearing off the fiber along the grain of the tree (fig. 2) and the inner bark, thus it will look more natural. The cambium cell layer and sapwood should also be removed.

An engraving machine may help to make it easier to carve those thick and large branches (fig. 3) before gravers are used for detailed carving. Then use sandpaper to remove the tool marks so that it is natural-looking.

Only proceed with carving the tree when you are sure of your design, because the removed bark can never be undone. The best time to create a *sheli* penjing is when the tree is at its dormant state, rather than in summer when the tree grows fast.

Fig. 1 Natural *sheli* in the wild. Some branches of this juniper in the Grand Canyon National Park have already died or withered due to external damage from extreme weather conditions, forming a compelling contrast with signs of life of the living twigs.

Fig. 2 Tearing off the fiber along the grain of the tree.

Fig. 3 Working with an engraving machine.

Vicissitudes of Life
Species: *Juniperus chinensis* (Chinese Juniper)
Age of tree: 120 years old
Height of tree: 70 cm
Container: Rectangular sandy clay tray
Designer: Zhao Qingquan
Introduction: The evergreen Chinese Juniper has a very long life span. It usually has a short trunk and looks old. The source tree was first trained in the wild. It was cut back to 70 cm and carefully carved in early 1980s when it was over 130 cm tall. Part of the *sheli* was natural dead wood. The brown living veins in the front of the trunk running along the *sheli* part makes the viewer wonder what it has experienced in its life.

Fig. 1 Natural rock peaks in the wild (Huangshan Mountain, Anhui Province).

Fig. 2 Natural rocks in the wild (Jinbian River, Zhangjiajie, Hunan Province).

Fig. 3 Peaks in *The Mustard Seed Garden Painting Manual*.

Fig. 4 Rocks in *The Mustard Seed Garden Painting Manual*.

Rocks

In Chinese culture, it is said that rocks make mountains attractive, waters limpid, gardens beautiful, and houses elegant. While most penjing benefit from rock accents, an ideal landscape penjing is created using rocks as the main artistic medium. In water and land penjing, rocks are only second to trees in its composition. In tree penjing, rocks can also be used as a supportive design element to accompany or enhance trees. Of course, for the category called "trees in rocks," the two ingredients are equally important.

Selection

Rocks can be soft and hard by nature. Soft rocks such as sedimentary sandstone are porous enough to allow percolation of water and are easy to work with. However, they are used less and less by penjing artists because they lack the strong rock flavor associated with durability. There are many types of hard rocks with various shapes, qualities, and colors. They add greatly to the naturalness of penjing specimens. When choosing rocks for your penjing, try to think how the shapes, qualities, and colors of the materials are related to the theme of your work and how they can be arranged to form a natural looking composition.

In landscape penjing, mountain landscape–peaks, ranges, hillocks, and even the foot of a hill–is composed solely of rocks. However, different rocks are chosen for different purposes. For example, thin and long rocks are ideal material for cliffs and peaks, but rocks with flat surfaces are good for the foot of a hill. In addition, markings and textures on hard rocks are also important in creating a mountain landscape because they are seldom carved into a particular shape. One category of rock is usually selected for a penjing, with similar but slightly varied

natural markings and textures.

In water and land penjing, rocks are mainly incorporated to feature river or creek banks and slopes, or interspersed rocks on a land mass rather than the panoramic view of mountains, so the "shapes" of rock are more important in the artist's consideration. A mountain landscape involves peaks, ranges, hillocks and valleys, while rocks are merely a small component of the whole view. The difference between a mountain landscape and a rock scene are well illustrated in Chinese landscape paintings (figures 1–4).

Shigan ("the nature of rock"), or the conventional image of a rock, can never be disregarded. Rocks are the main medium used to represent the "roughness" in a water and land penjing to contrast with the "gentleness" of other elements. In general, hard rocks are typically considered more "rock" than sedimentary sandstone. Of course, hard rocks that look soft are not standard rocks for penjing design. One category of rocks with similar shapes, qualities, markings, and colors are usually selected for a penjing. This of course does not mean they have to be exactly same; variations in surface size, texture, and shape contribute to the final harmonious composition.

The following are commonly used rocks in penjing art:

Turtle Shell Rock. This hard rock has interesting natural markings that resemble the patterns found on the shell of a turtle. Turtle Pattern Rocks can be grayish yellow, grayish black, light red, or white. They are porous rocks and allow mosses and lichens to grow. They can be carved and polished to a certain degree (fig. 5).

Turtle Pattern Rocks are simple, natural- and old-looking in shape and color, with a strong feeling of roughness, making them an ideal penjing material, especially for water and land landscapes.

Turtle Pattern Rocks are mainly available in Sichuan, Anhui, and Shandong provinces, but with different qualities, markings, and colors.

Ying Rock. Most Ying Rocks are hard and craggy, with rich and varied markings on them, although some can be round with fewer markings. They are not porous and are not easy to work. They are usually either grayish black or light gray, sometimes with white lines in them (fig. 6).

As a conventional type of hard rock, Ying Rocks from Guangdong Province are popular as ornamental stones in China and are common material for water and land penjing.

Cobblestones. Most cobblestones are small, smooth, egg-shaped, although some irregular shapes can also be found. These hard rocks with few markings are often black, white, gray, green or light brown. They are not porous and are not easy to work (fig. 7).

These conventional solid rocks are often glued together to represent riverbanks and slopes in water and land penjing, but those with irregular shapes and rich markings are more popular.

Cobblestones can be found in the streams, rivers, and the vicinity of old mining sites in many regions in China.

Stalagmite rock. Stalagmite rocks are hard and usually available in the shape of bamboo shoots. Some pieces contain gray-white shiny inclusions resembling ginkgo seeds. They are of many colors, ranging from grayish green to purple. They are not porous, but they are easy to bust into smaller pieces with a hammer. Stalagmite rocks are popular material in landscape penjing which feature rock cliffs, peaks, or stone forests. Grayish green stalagmites are ideal material to portray landscape featuring spring scenes (fig. 8).

Stalagmite rocks are available in Zhejiang Province in China.

Axe-split Rock. This rock is often available in long narrow strips. It can be grayish black, light gray, bluish black, or light

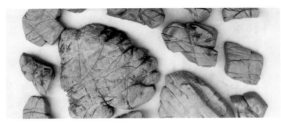
Fig. 5 Turtle Shell Rock.

Fig. 7 Cobblestones.

Fig. 9 Axe-split Rock.

Fig. 6 Ying Rock.

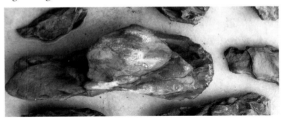
Fig. 8 Stalagmite rock.

Fig. 10 Petrified wood.

Fig. 11 Taihu rock.

brown, depending on when it was formed, to what degree it has been weathered, and what it is composed of. Pure rocks of light gray without foreign substances are among the best for penjing composition (fig. 9).

Axe-split Rocks are solid with straight markings. They are often best used in landscape penjing to represent magnificent, powering, and steep peaks.

They are mainly available in Jiangsu Province in China.

Petrified wood. It is the fossil of wood that has turned to stone through the process of silicification or calcification. While it maintains the original features of the wood, it is firm and crisp, and has a very low water absorption capacity. Petrified wood is an ideal medium to feature lofty and towering peaks or cliffs. Petrified wood is found in a variety of regions in China (fig. 10).

Taihu rock. Taihu rocks are formed by continuous erosive actions of lake water and waves. The colors are generally grayish white, light gray, or grayish black. These limestone rocks are very hard, and they are often incorporated as what they are. The rocks often have mild curvy edges and their surfaces are usually covered with perforations. The rocks in the wild are usually very large, and those that are small enough to be suitable for penjing compositions are not found easily (fig. 11).

Taihu rocks are mainly from Taihu Lake, Jiangsu Province, and Chaohu Lake, Anhui Province.

Fig. 1 A rock to be placed as shorelines or slopes needs to have a flattened bottom.

Fig. 2 Working with a stone cutter.

Fig. 3 Chiseling a rock.

Fig. 4 Polishing rock with waterproof sandpaper.

Fig. 5 Cementing two pieces of rock.

Cutting and Polishing

You often have to work with the rocks to be incorporated in a landscape or a water and land penjing. The work may involve cutting, chiseling, polishing, or cementing processes, according to the specific category of the rock and the requirement of the whole design.

Cutting. Unwanted parts of a piece of rock may have to be removed for a specific purpose. For example, rocks to be placed as shorelines or slopes need to be flattened so that they can be affixed on the bottom of the container naturally and without gaps between them (fig. 1). Sometimes a rock is broken into several pieces. Interspersed rocks on land mass are seldom cut, but part of a large one that sometimes does need to be removed.

Hard rocks need to be carefully and repeatedly examined to decide upon the best way to work with them. Soft rocks are often chiseled before they are cut.

To cut rocks neatly, you may need a rock cutter. It is important during cutting to protect the edges not to be broken. In addition, always take safety precautions and wear proper safety equipment while operating machinery (fig. 2).

Chiseling. Unsatisfactory soft rocks can be shaped with a chisel or a pointed hammer (fig. 3).

Rocks need to be chiseled in a manner so that they are natural looking. While the shapes and markings in traditional Chinese painting serve as a good reference, you will benefit greatly from observing natural landscapes. Rocks in a landscape penjing should be similar in style, but variations are necessary.

Polishing. Surfaces of a rock are often polished by using a polisher or waterproof sandpaper to remove tool marks or edges, or to make up for drawbacks in the rocks. For rocks with nice natural shapes, polishing should be performed as less as possible to retain the natural feel of them. When polishing a rock surface, it is better to use a polishing machine with a coarse abrasive disc first and then manually polish the surface again with fine sandpaper (fig. 4).

Cementing. Cementing two or more pieces of rock together to form a whole is a technique commonly used in landscape and water and land penjing building. Shorelines and slopes are often landscaped with several rocks (fig. 5).

A sense of the entirety of the work is essential in cementing rocks for a landscape. First, the rocks to be glued together need to be similar in color and pattern of markings. Second, they should be well attached to each other to be structurally coherent. Finally, glue them carefully with cement. Rocks cemented together should have an overall sense of harmony in color, pattern of markings, size, and shape, but at the same time, they need to vary slightly in these aspects, thus achieving diversity and unity.

Fig. 6 This is a detail of the water and land penjing entitled *Cowboys in Spring* by Zhao Qingquan. Well-chosen and well-placed miniatures can artistically enhance a landscape composition, adding liveliness to the scene.

Miniatures

Miniatures in penjing refer to small structures, figurines, animals, boats, or other complimentary accents added to a design. Well-chosen and well-placed miniatures can artistically enhance a landscape composition, adding liveliness to the scene or featuring elements of the season, region, and times. They help to develop a specific theme (fig. 6). At the same time, they help to establish a sense of proportion to reveal the sizes of the trees, rocks, and other design elements. For example, the smaller a miniature is, the larger a nearby tree or rock is. When miniatures at the back are normally smaller than those in the front, they give depth to a scene.

However, these accessories are never mandatory for all water and land penjing, and the number of them that are needed vary from specimen with different themes. Generally, they are used sparingly, tastefully, and artistically, and they should never dominate the composition. Inappropriateness in size and color of a miniature will distract the viewer.

While miniatures can be made of pottery, stone or metal, pottery structures and figurines are often popular due to their ability in retaining color when exposed to the sun and rain and achieving harmony easily with other natural materials. The following is a list of pottery miniatures commonly used.

Structures. Thatched pavilions, thatched houses, tile-roofed houses, waterside pavilions, stone slab bridges, plank bridges, bamboo bridge, etc. (fig. 7).

Figurines. Single person standing, sitting, or reading, two persons playing a game of Go, chatting, or drinking, man or men playing *qin* (a stringed musical instrument) or Chinese flute, man on back of a bull, fishermen, farmers, woodcutters, etc. (figures 8–9).

Animals. Bulls, horses, goats, cranes, chickens, ducks, and geese in different actions (fig. 10).

Boats. Sailing boats, sculling boats, fishing boats, ferryboats, bamboo rafts, etc. (fig. 11).

While these accents are available in penjing shops, designers sometimes make their own miniatures with wood, bamboo, stone or other natural materials, such as thatched pavilions, thatched houses, stone slab bridges, plank bridges, bamboo bridges, sailing boats, and bamboo rafts, according to their own designs. This allows them to realize their conceptions, better express the themes of their work, and add individuality to their composition.

Fig. 7 Miniature structures.

Fig. 8 Figurines in traditional Chinese clothes.

Fig. 9 Miniature cowboys.

Fig. 10 Miniature animals.

Fig. 11 Miniature boats.

Containers

The container to a penjing artist is what paper is to a painter, because penjing can be referred to as a three-dimensional Chinese painting. While pots or trays are necessary in penjing for holding the plants or rocks, they are also part of your whole design. A leader in pottery industry since ancient times, the Chinese have devised important techniques for penjing containers.

The containers for penjing can be with or without drainage holes (hence the names of "land pots" and "water pots"), for different penjing specimens. Those with drainage holes are mainly for tree penjing and those shallower without drainage holes are for landscape penjing. The latter is also used for water and land penjing, but holes are often available at the base of the "land" part.

"Land pots" of various colors and shapes are available in sandy clay ware, glazed pottery, or porcelain. They can also be made out of a piece of stone. Of course, some natural slabs of rock serve as excellent containers for penjing specimens.

Sandy clay containers. They are made of a special sandy clay from Yixing in Jiangsu Province, at the temperature of over 1,000°C. Different temperature ranges in the kiln result in various textures and colors, ranging from red, purple, green, beige, blue, green and black.

Sandy clay containers of various shapes have been made, usually without glazing. The fine nature and ability of water absorption make them ideal containers for potted plants.

These rustic and earthy containers are perfect foils for pines and junipers.

Glazed pottery containers. From Shiwan in Guangdong Province and Yixing in Jiangsu Province, they are of various shapes and known for their bright colors, and they are often used for leaf-, flower-, or fruit effect penjing trees and plants.

Stone containers. They are made out of white or light gray marble, cipolin, or granite. They are suitable to be used as water pots, but sometimes are also used as land pots. These containers are often rectangular, square or oval pots or trays.

Stone containers are produced in many places in China, including Yunnan, Shandong, Jiangsu, Sichuan provinces and Shanghai.

Natural stone slabs. They can function, sometimes after some polishing work, as good containers for landscape or water and land penjing due to their irregular shapes. Being almost flat, they do not hold water, but the penjing can be designed as if there was water in it.

"Water pots," containers with holes, can only be made of stone or glazed pottery, and their colors are mainly white, light

Glazed Pottery Containers

An oval glazed pottery tray

A square glazed pottery pot

A round petal-whorl-shaped glazed pottery tray

A rectangular glazed pottery tray

A Chinese-crabapple-shaped glazed pottery pot

A Chinese-crabapple-shaped glazed pottery pot

gray, light blue and light green, which are chosen according to the theme and color of rocks selected. Penjing featuring seas, lakes, snow, and night scenes are often placed in light blue, light green, white, and black containers, respectively.

Most water pots or trays are rectangular or oval and with plain shapes which are not decorated with any lines or patterns. The ideal dimensions of the pot depend on the depth of the scene. The majority of pots or trays are twice as long as they are wide, while square or round containers can be selected to show the great depth of a scene. Long narrow rectangular or boat-shaped containers are perfect foils for the effect of a long scroll Chinese painting.

The proportion between the size of the pot and the height of the scene varies from design to design in accordance with the artistic expression and there are no prescribed rules for penjing artists.

Stone Containers

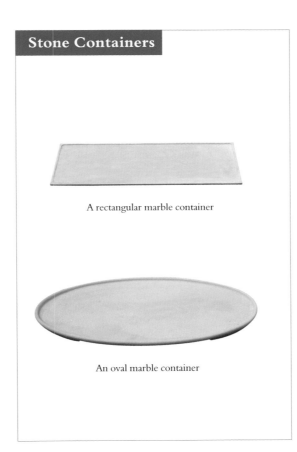

A rectangular marble container

An oval marble container

Natural Stone Slabs

A natural stone container

Legend has it that this natural container of dripstone was left by a group of people who searched for bizarre rocks for a Song dynasty emperor when they were in Yangzhou. It is now displayed in the Slender West Lake in Yangzhou.

Sandy Clay Containers

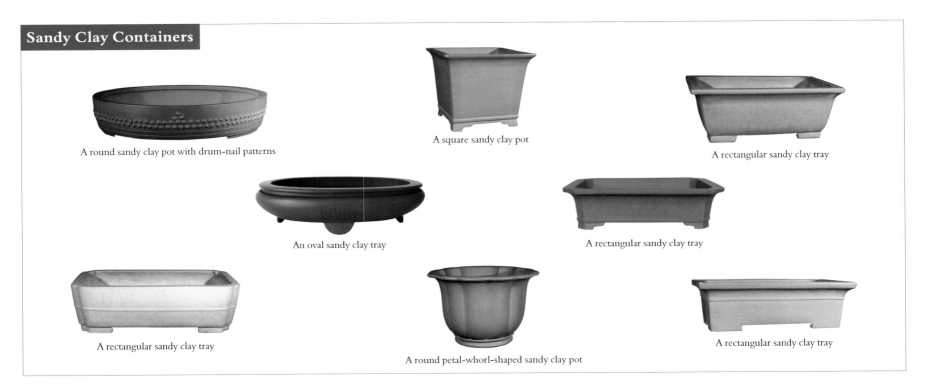

A round sandy clay pot with drum-nail patterns

A square sandy clay pot

A rectangular sandy clay tray

An oval sandy clay tray

A rectangular sandy clay tray

A rectangular sandy clay tray

A round petal-whorl-shaped sandy clay pot

A rectangular sandy clay tray

CHAPTER FOUR
CATEGORIES AND DESIGNS

Chinese penjing generally fall into one of three categories classified by source material, subject matter, and design: tree penjing, landscape penjing, and water and land penjing.

Tree penjing depicts in pots the image of natural trees and plants, as the dominant elements in the composition are wired, pruned, chiseled to create aesthetically pleasing images. Tree penjing is often classified as "single-tree penjing," which features a single tree, and "forest penjing," which comprises the planting of two or more trees.

Landscape penjing specimens feature mountains and water in shallow water pot by cutting, chiseling, and reshaping carefully chosen rocks. There are two types according to the nature of the rocks used in the design: hard-rock penjing and soft-rock penjing (see page 67).

Water and land penjing is a hybrid of the previous two types that depicts not only a landscape consisting of mountains and water, but also the images of trees and plants with source materials that may include plants, rocks, soil, and water. While specimens may feature a single tree, there are well-established style categories for specimens with two or more trunks (see page 66).

A tentative layout concerning the theme, shape, layout, and style of the penjing to be created is necessary before you begin your work. It is the key to any successful composition. Without an advance conception, any effort would lead to waste or loss of the materials chosen.

Conceptions of penjing design are based on natural scenes, but with reference to guidelines in Chinese landscape painting. One of the best methods that can be tried beforehand is to figure out what elements can be best exploited in your source materials–trees, rocks, pots, and miniatures–to develop your theme, and what else is needed to better your design. With a preliminary design in mind, you can start to work with a reasonable degree of assurance for success.

Early Spring
Species: *Tamarix chinensis* (Chinese Tamarisk)
Type of rock: Turtle Shell Rock
Container: Rectangular marble tray
Length of container: 90 cm
Designer: Yao Naigong
Introduction: This is a Chinese Tamarisk water and land penjing. The featured specimen is Chinese Tamarisk in the spring. The composition shows excellent contrast between the two trees in dominance, height, and movement.

Natural willow trees. The landscape in the Slender West Lake can be regarded as a water and land penjing created by nature.

Lijiang River
Type of rock: Sandstone
Container: Oval marble tray
Length of container: 150 cm
Designer: Zhao Qingquan
Introduction: This is a landscape penjing built with sandstone. This specimen portrays a typical landscape along the Lijiang River by cementing several pieces of natural sandstone. The opening-and-closing style penjing shows excellent contrasts between dominance and subordination, as well as emptiness and substance.

This landscape along the Lijiang River in Guilin, Guangxi Province, is often portrayed in landscape penjing specimens.

Eight Relations for Designing

Like masterpieces in Chinese poetry and ink painting, great penjing specimens engage the viewers and draw them into the composition, providing them much food for thought. However, simply following the guidelines in penjing reference books alone will not guarantee success in creating work with artistic values—your design is greatly aided by observing natural landscapes. At the same time, principles for artistic creation need to be adhered to, and artistic and creative techniques need to be employed to deal with the relationships between the eight pairs of opposites: dominance and subordination, emptiness and substance, denseness and sparseness, roughness and meticulousness, firmness and gentleness, entirety and individuality, lightness and heaviness, and feelings and scene. Only in this way do penjing artists' goal to pursue variety in harmony can be achieved.

One Dominance and Subordination

It is important in penjing design to highlight the dominant feature. There is only one component that dominates the whole composition, to which all the others are subordinate. So various techniques should be employed to distinguish the dominant from the subordinate, otherwise the composition must be dull and boring.

Enjoying Nature
Species: *Ulmus parvifolia* (Chinese Elm)
Age of (main) tree: 60 years old
Container: Rectangular marble tray
Length of container: 120 cm
Designer: Zheng Yongtai
Introduction: Sense of dominance and subordination in tree penjing. The two contrasting Chinese Elm trees have been trained from earlier stumps. The original stumps are like two mounds, on which the small trees grow. While the largest elm dominates the composition, others are subordinate but vary in size and height, forming a dynamic entirety.

68

Road to Sichuan
Type of rock: Quartzite from Xinjiang
Container: Oval marble tray
Length of container: 90 cm
Designer: Qiao Honggen
Introduction: Sense of dominance and subordination in landscape penjing. In this landscape penjing that has several peaks, the dominant peak is always the tallest and the largest. The main peak and the accompanying rocks are carefully orchestrated to complement each other and give emphasis to a highly dynamic composition.

An Old Tree over a Pond
Species: *Ulmus parvifolia* (Chinese Elm)
Age of tree: 50 years old
Type of rock: Turtle Shell Rock
Container: Oval marble tray
Length of container: 140 cm
Designer: Zhao Qingquan
Introduction: Sense of dominance and subordination in water and land penjing. In this specimen, the tree dominates the composition, while the rocks are the accents. The main tree is the largest one, to which others are subordinate. All components are arranged in such a way that they form an entirety, but with variations.

69

Contrasts in foliage between emptiness and substance, and between denseness and sparseness. This is a detail of *Drinking Horse* (see the title-page for more details).

To highlight the main dominant feature, its shape, location, and size should be decided before all others are taken into consideration.

It has to be noted that the relationship between dominance and subordination is not an absolute one. While only one feature dominates the whole composition, there is always a leading component in a visibly separate section.

Two Emptiness and Substance

Chinese classical philosophy holds that the world is a blend of emptiness and substance. As emptiness (void) and substance are born by each other, they also reside in each other. The relationship between emptiness and substance is highlighted in traditional Chinese art in poetry, literature, opera, painting, dance, music, calligraphy, and gardening. To represent the essence and nature of the world in a realistic and dynamic manner, artists should observe the guideline that emptiness and substance are born by each other.

In a design of penjing, the balance between emptiness and substance can be understood as of that between being and non-being, which are relatively, rather than absolutely, related.

In tree penjing, such relationships exist between trunks and foliage, trees and space, and trees and container. As a general guideline, space is empty while trunks are examples of substance. However, foliage is empty in contrast to trunks, but they are matters of substance to empty spaces. Structurally, sparse parts are representations of emptiness, and dense parts realize substance.

In landscape penjing, empty spaces–parts of a composition that has nothing showing–are realizations of emptiness. They are important components of the landscape, representing water, clouds or sky.

The sense of emptiness and substance in water and land penjing is more complex, because more elements—tree, rock, water, land—are often incorporated. Compared with empty spaces, landscapes are representations of substance. In the same manner, rocks and trees are realizations of substance, in contrast to water, which is on the empty side. However, compared with rocks, trees are empty. In an idealized penjing, emptiness and substance co-exist in each other and are created by each other.

70

Inquiring of the Moon
Species: *Pinus parviflora*
(Japanese Five Needle Pine)
Age of tree: 35 years old
Height of tree: 100 cm
Container: Petal-whorl-shaped
sandy clay pot
Designer: Xu Ronglin
Introduction: Sense of
emptiness and substance in
literati penjing. Literati penjing
features simple structures,
and the sense of emptiness
and substance is all the more
important. With a clear structure
and sparse foliage, the specimen
leaves much empty space to
allow the viewer's imagination
to run wild.

71

Mist-covered Water

Species: *Ligustrum quihoui* (Quihoui privet) and *Punica granatum* (Pomegranate)
Age of (main) tree: 8 years old
Type of rock: Turtle Shell Rock
Container: Oval marble tray
Length of container: 100 cm
Designer: Zhao Qingquan
Introduction: Sense of emptiness and substance in water and land penjing. Compared
with the empty spaces, the landscape in the specimen is the representation of
substance. In the same manner, the rocks and trees are realizations of substance, in
contrast to the water, which is in the empty side. However, compared with the rocks,
the trees are emptier. In this penjing, emptiness and substance reside in each other and
are created by each other.

A sense of denseness and sparseness of interspersed rocks in water and land penjing. This is a detail of the penjing entitled *Woodcutter* (see page 76 for a more detailed introduction to it). The interspersed rocks vary in size and are well spaced.

Three Denseness and Sparseness

The contrast between denseness and sparseness is a structural consideration in traditional Chinese art.

The balance between denseness and sparseness should be well kept in a penjing design and layout. While viewers may feel nervous and even depressed before a landscape that is tightly packed, those that are too sparse lack energy and tension. While denseness and sparseness in penjing art are relative, they reinforce and enhance each other by the sharp contrast between them. As every piece of art work impresses people by its inner rhythms, a well-spaced penjing specimen has its own musical rhythms.

The balance between denseness and sparseness gives the viewer the impression of a forest when there are only a couple of miniature trees present. However, the same trees lined up evenly in a container would never impress the viewer in the same fashion, because trees in the wild are never spaced so neatly.

But how do you balance denseness and sparseness in a design? A rule of thumb is that features are arranged to show alternative effects of denseness and sparseness. To be more specific, a proper contrast between denseness and sparseness should be recognized between trees, branches, exposed roots, markings on rocks, positions of rocks, and parts of shorelines. At the same time, denseness should be seen in a sparse part, while sparseness is felt in a dense section. Generalities are hard to list as to which part should highlight denseness or sparseness, and to what degree. They are often matters of personal preference at the artist's discretion.

Spring
Species: *Taxodium distichum* (Bald Cypress)
Container: Rectangular glazed pottery tray
Length of container: 150 cm
Designer: Han Xuenian
Introduction: Sense of denseness and sparseness in forest penjing. More than 100 seedlings of Bald Cypresses are arranged in this forest to complement each other and give rise to a natural and highly dynamic composition. The contrast between sparseness and denseness best features the sense of spring.

An Old Man in Spring
Species: *Stranvaesia davidiana* (Chinese Stranvaesia)
Age of tree: 40 years old
Height of tree: 180 cm
Container: Rectangular sandy clay tray
Designer: Wu Chengfa
Introduction: Sense of denseness and sparseness in tree penjing. This specimen represents the inner rhythms of trees by the shapes of the trunk and branches of the tree and a clear sense of denseness and sparseness.

Peaks in Cloud
Type of rock: Xixia Rock
Container: Oval marble tray
Length of container: 90 cm
Designer: Qiao Honggen
Introduction: Sense of denseness and sparseness in landscape penjing. This opening-and-closing style landscape penjing has a wider opening in the front. The dominant part on the left has more rocks than other parts. The empty space in the middle displays a lively nature by stirring the imagination.

Clear Creek
Species: *Pseudolarix amabilis* (Golden Larch)
Container: Oval marble tray
Length of container: 90 cm
Designer: Zhao Qingquan
Introduction: Sense of denseness and sparseness in forest penjing. This forest penjing consists of many single-trunk Golden Larch trees. The main tree serves as the focal point of the composition; other trees are spaced to show a clear sense of sparseness and denseness, which helps to give the viewer the impression of a large forest and to add a musical rhythm to the composition.

Vigor
Species: *Ulmus parvifolia*
(Chinese Elm)
Age of tree: 60 years old
Height of tree: 76 cm
Container: Rectangular glazed
pottery tray
Designer: Zhao Qingquan
Introduction: Roughness and
meticulousness in tree shaping.
This Chinese Elm penjing
permeates the vigor of huge
elms in the wild in every inch
of its trunk, branches, and even
new growth.

Woodcutter
Species: *Ulmus parvifolia*
(Chinese Elm)
Age of (main) tree: 30 years old
Type of rock: Turtle Shell Rock
Container: Oval marble tray
Length of container: 120 cm
Designer: Zhao Qingquan
Introduction: Sense of
roughness and meticulousness
in water and land penjing. This
penjing consists of several trees
of various sizes. The main
tree is the largest, balanced
with smaller trees to give rise
to a highly natural, dynamic
composition.

Four Roughness and Meticulousness

Roughness and meticulousness in penjing does not only refer to the qualities of lines and shapes of a landscape, but are also used to describe devices of expression and work on source materials as well as styles.

A penjing shaped too roughly would have no focus and lack contrasts between components, but one with too much detail would be a boring soulless structure. An idealized specimen is always a blend featuring both roughness and meticulousness, emphasizing its focus while benefiting from contrasts between facets. While different styles of penjing vary in their preference to roughness or meticulousness, the two always co-exist in any masterpiece, either as a dominant or subordinate feature.

The arrangement of a penjing usually starts with its overall layout, rather than details of individual components and complementary features, which can only be taken into account when you are satisfied with the layout. This helps to give you a sense of entirety, which decides in what manner and with what rhythms you are going to represent your theme in details.

When shaping a tree, the structures and movements of the trunk and primary branches should be decided before smaller branches are trimmed. To create a rock landscape, you need to be sure about its shape and the main rock, and then proceed with the detailed cutting and polishing processes, although you may want to fine tune the structure as you work on the details. In this way you work under the guidance of a sense of entirety when you are trying to highlight a feature in a part of the scene.

Gorges
Type of rock: Phosphate rock
Container: Oval marble tray
Length of container: 150 cm
Designer: Rui Xinhua
Introduction: Sense of roughness and meticulousness in landscape penjing. Larger rocks with thick lines are used by the artist to represent the imposing grandeur of the gorges, but this artistic roughness is well balanced by small trees on the rocks, streams in the hill, and sailing boats in the water, forming a dynamic composition with a clear sense of roughness and meticulousness.

Five Firmness and Gentleness

Nature keeps its balance between firmness and gentleness by stark contrasts between natural things such as powering mountains and zigzagging rivers, and straight and tall pines and charming willows. These different landscapes contribute to the varied but harmonious world.

The relationship between firmness and gentleness in a penjing needs to be reflected in its theme, style, shape, and source materials. In terms of theme and style, some specimens best feature their characteristic of firmness, while others benefit from their realization of gentleness. In terms of artistic shape, techniques are often used to show a blend of firmness and gentleness in a specimen, but with various emphasis on each of them. As for components, rocks and trees, as well as rocks and rocks, are often contrasted to feature firmness and gentleness. Trees themselves show the difference by their contrast between straight and curved trunks or branches, or between shape and gentle curves in them.

Two Dragons over a Valley
Species: *Sageretia theezans*
(Chinese Bird Plum)
Age of tree: 40 years old
Spread: 100 cm
Container: Round glazed
pottery tray
Designer: Han Xuenian
Introduction: Sense of firmness
and gentleness in tree branches.
Traditional Chinese art
highlights lines. This cliff-style
penjing looks like two dragons
over a deep valley, with a variety
of line shapes.

Fisherman
Species: *Sageretia theezans* (Chinese Bird Plum)
Age of (main) tree: 40 years old
Type of rock: Turtle Shell Rock
Container: Oval marble tray
Length of container: 120 cm
Designer: Zhao Qingquan
Introduction: Sense of elements echoing with one another in water and land penjing. The work consists of two visible parts; the major on the right and the accent on the left. The main branches of the trees, however, progress toward each other. The same species of the tree and similar shape of the rocks contribute to the harmony of the composition as a whole.

Six Entirety and Individuality

The components in water and land penjing—tree, rock, water, land mass, and miniature—are never isolated items, but are chosen with an eye toward their ability to contribute to the whole design. No matter if they are dominate features or not, they are realizations of emptiness or substance or representations of denseness and sparseness. Each and every element in the design needs to relate to all the others so that the entire landscape appears a complete entity. Such relationships are usually achieved by a balance of movement.

The balance of movement can be realized by placing components in a similar direction such as the direction to which the primary branch extends or rocks lean. Complementary accents should have a similar movement with the dominant feature. All subordinate items can also be arranged so that they "move" toward the main feature.

The balance of movement with the dominant feature can also be represented in categories, shapes, lines, and colors of components, as well as degrees of denseness, emptiness, and heaviness in design. For example, if the main tree is straight and upright, other trees should be in similar shapes so that they have a similar movement. When the dominant feature is mainly of a particular color, the same color should be seen in other components. A large piece of rock should be accompanied with several smaller rocks, and a part in the composition which has nothing showing would seem isolated if no similar arrangements are found in the rest of the design. In this way all components of the composition are linked and complementary to each other.

Sailing out the Gorges
Type of rock: Axe-split Rock
Container: Oval marble tray
Length of container: 150 cm
Designer: Zhao Qingquan
Introduction: Sense of elements echoing with one another in landscape penjing. This penjing features a gorge landscape. The peaks are artistically orchestrated to complement each other by using rocks with similar shapes and markings and give rise to a highly dynamic entirety.

Trees and small plants may be incorporated as accents in the design of water and land penjing. This is a detail of *Mist-covered Water* (see page 72 for a more detailed introduction). The sense of lightness and heaviness is achieved by the sparse forest with small trees and large rocks.

Seven Lightness and Heaviness

When we look at things in daily life, we have a sense of their lightness or heaviness based on our experience. The same is true of the components in a penjing specimen. This sense of lightness or heaviness is solely psychological and it has nothing to do with the weight of a particular item. To please the viewer with this psychological effect, a good balance between lightness and heaviness should be maintained in the composition.

An asymmetrical balance is required for penjing composition. For example, the dominant component is usually placed slightly off center from the mid-point lines; more components are found at one side of the container; the branches are shorter and leaves are denser on the one side than the other; large and dense foliage are often balanced with whorled roots exposed above the soil surface and a large container. In addition, interspersed rocks and small miniatures can also be placed in the empty space for better balance.

It has to be noted that the relationship between lightness and heaviness is relative. While the contrast is sharp in some parts, it is not so obvious in other places. However, as a general guideline, rocks are heavier than trees, which carries more heaviness with them than water, while blank space is the lightest among them; scenes closer to the viewer are heavier than those that are located back further; sparse landscapes are lighter than compacted ones; thicker lines are heavier than thin ones; and subdued colors are lighter than dark ones.

These are only general guidelines and they are not absolute. Sometimes they are used differently or even the opposite may be true. It depends on what the penjing artist is trying to convey.

Shade in Summer
Species: *Musa cavendishii*-Banana (Chinese Banana)
Container: Curvy-lipped marble tray
Length of container: 100 cm
Designer: Zheng Yongtai
Introduction: This is a forest with several young Chinese Bananas. The seedlings with large leaves balance the incorporated small pieces of rock on the surface of the soil. Rocks may be used as supportive design elements in tree penjing.

Large and small rocks in water and land penjing. This is a detail of the penjing *Water Running on Rocks* (see page 101 for a more detailed introduction to it).

Camels and the Sea
Type of rock: Wind-eroded rock
Container: Oval marble tray
Length of container: 120 cm
Designer: Qiao Honggen
Introduction: Sense of primary and secondary peaks in landscape penjing. The smaller and lower peaks on the right not only highlight the primary peaks on the left through contrast, but also contribute to the balance of heaviness and lightness in the whole composition.

Eight Emotion and Scene

A penjing artist takes advantage of a scene he is building to express his own emotions. Idealized penjing specimens not only engage the viewer, but also encourage them to go beyond the surface by stirring their imagination and emotions. It is mainly through the fusion of emotions with limited natural landscape that images are created in penjing art.

Each and every component in the composition is imbued with the artist's unique view of the world and his affection for nature. This is why the viewer may go beyond the surface landscape to allow their imagination to run and express their emotions. This is what it means by "fusion of emotions with landscape."

To achieve this goal, penjing artists first need to have affection for life and nature. It is believed in aesthetics of traditional Chinese painting that "characteristics and affections of mountains and water are those of mine..., and painter need to have these characteristics and affections." Painters are often advised not to draw what they see with their eyes but what they feel with their heart. Penjing art is no exception. Artists who lack affection for nature and beauty would never infuse their work with a depth of emotions and energy. Second, perfect penjing are created by following the general rules that govern the art, and benefit from creative use of various techniques commonly applied in the field.

Furthermore, a good title for your work would add the touch that brings it to life. Titling is a way of expression in Chinese painting, but is employed in penjing art as well. With elegant titles appropriately conceived, many penjing specimens are endowed with more impressing poetic images. The title of a penjing specimen is often composed according to what the artist is trying to convey and what image is contained in the work. It can be the artist's own creation or a quotation or an adaptation from an ancient Chinese poem. Illusions from literary works and paintings serve as another source for penjing artists.

The best penjing titles are always concise but informative, and their language needs to be graceful, vivid, and rhythmic.

Forest in the Distance
Species: *Pseudolarix amabilis* (Golden Larch)
Type of rock: Turtle Shell Rock
Container: Oval marble tray
Length of container: 90 cm
Designer: Zhao Qingquan
Introduction: Sense of emotion and scene. The forest-style water and land penjing specimen describes a scene portrayed in a Tang poem: a person filled with worries is standing on the balcony of a building with his eyes fixed upon a misty forest in the distance.

Natural pines in the wild (Lushan Mountains, Jiangxi Province).

Broad-leaved tree in the wild.

Natural trees growing in rocks (Central Park, New York, USA).

Penjing that features a single tree is called "single-tree penjing," and penjing that is comprised of two or more planted trees is a "forest penjing".

Tree penjing is greatly aided by observation of natural trees created by nature in different environments.

Single-tree Penjing

Single-tree penjing is by far the most commonly seen type of tree penjing, which highlights an individual tree in the natural landscape. The artist often features trees of different categories in different conditions: a pine on a hill, an old tree in a highland, a woody plant by a river. Trees growing in different environments, even of the same species, will have different shapes.

The techniques of single-tree penjing are a good start for beginners to familiarize themselves with the basics of tree penjing before they learn to design forest penjing.

Shape

The "front" of the tree, the most beautiful side to be displayed, must be chosen first. At the direct front of the ideal tree for a penjing, the trunk does not bend in the direction of the viewer, and the exposed roots and primary branches progress more at the two sides. The side of the trunk facing the viewer should never be bare or with long branches. The primary branches should be without parallel or symmetrical sub-branches and progress in different layers. When the trunk is with visible curves, the primary branches should grow at the outside of a curve.

Unfortunately, in many cases designers find themselves in a dilemma: while the exposed roots look great, the trunk is not pleasing or vice versa. Then a decision must have to be made as to whether measures can be taken to make up the drawbacks.

The movement of each tree, i.e. the direction of its trunk, roots, and branches is critical. When you have decided upon the "front" of a tree, try different movements to see which one best expresses what you are trying to represent. A small change in the movement of a tree sometimes makes a difference to a penjing.

The next step is to think about the lengths, density, spacing, firmness, and movements of primary branches, which is followed by adjustments of the basic structure and shape of the trees.

Styles

Straight-trunk style. Penjing trees are characterized by a straight, upright, tapering trunk, with layers of straight protruding or drooping branches, mimicking old domineering trees in the wild. Straight trunk tree penjing can be designed with one or more trunks (see page 88, left).

Slanting-trunk style. The slanting trunk, with visible curves, emerges from the soil at an angle, but the primary branches progress in the opposite direction in a dynamic manner, infused with the characteristics of unrestraint and refined elegance of old trees in the wild. They can also be designed with one or more trunks (see page 88, right).

Cascade style. With the trunk sticking out the tray and the apex extending along it, a cascade-style specimen is modeled after trees that grow over water. Like a Chinese painting, it is full of naturalness and elegance (see page 89).

Cliff-hanging style. The trunk in the cliff-hanging style penjing extends well beneath the lip of the penjing pot, while the branches progress upward, as if an old pine whose roots grow in soil contained within the cracks and holes of a rock on a cliff. This style is imbued with the spirit of courage in a dangerous situation (see page 90).

Curved-trunk style. In this style the trunk progress like a tortuous dragon, with layers of well-arranged branches and leaves (see page 64).

Interlocking-root style. With exposed roots of a couple of trees coiled into bizarre shapes on the container surfaces, the trunks and branches progress to varying heights. The style features tree with interlocking roots in the wild (see page 91).

Weeping style. With slanting or curving trunks, drooping branch style penjing have long thin branches that hang down, representing characteristics of aloofness and elegance of trees, such as weeping willows (see page 92).

Windswept style. This style features a penjing tree with a trunk and primary branches of an ordinary tree, but with thinner branches progressing in one direction as if the tree is affected by strong winds blowing continuously. The trunk can be upright, slanting or with curves (see page 93).

Root-in-rock style. This style means the roots of the tree are growing in soil contained within the cracks and holes of the rock, portraying old trees that grow in rocks or on cliffs (see pages 94–95).

Literati style. Literati style does not contrast with any of the preceding categories. It can be shaped with slanting, curved, or an upright trunk or trunks; the tree or trees can be on a cliff or at a riverside. It can be designed with one or more trunks (see pages 96–98).

It is characterized by a thin trunk, with few branches and sparse leaves on the top. Rather than portraying a tree in the wild, the style is imbued with the characteristics of aloofness of scholars; hence "literati style." It is a style which requires much cultural training.

Against Cloud and the Sun
Species: *Pinus parviflora* (Japanese Five Needle Pine)
Age of tree: 150 years old
Height of tree: 76 cm
Container: Rectangular sandy clay tray
Collector: Shanghai Botanical Garden
Introduction: Aged as it is, this Japanese Five Needle Pine penjing has a striking shape with excellent structures, and lines in its green and luxuriant foliage.

Gorgeous Summer Scene
Species: *Punica granatum* (Pomegranate)
Age of tree: 45 years old
Height of tree: 60 cm
Container: Rectangular glazed pottery tray
Designer: Wang Xin
Introduction: The specimen is straight-trunk style; it has an upright trunk and dense foliage, featuring the imposing grandeur of naturally large trees. The snow-white glazed pottery tray contrasts well with the fiery red flowers.

Moon Fairy
Species: *Podocarpus macrophyllus var. maki* (Yew Plum)
Age of tree: 70 years old
Height of tree: 52 cm
Container: Rectangular sandy clay tray
Designer: Zhao Qingquan
Introduction: This is slanting-trunk style. The trunk of the Yew Plum leans toward the right with a slight curve, but the foliage progress in the opposite direction, forming a balanced but dynamic entirety.

The Dragon
Species: *Buxus sinica* (Chinese Box)
Age of tree: 60 years old
Spread: 56 cm
Container: Round vase-shaped glazed pottery pot
Designer: Zhao Qingquan
Introduction: This is cascade style. With a curved trunk and a crown extending out of the container, the specimen looks like a flying dragon. The leaves grow above and under the trunk, showing a natural grace and unrestrained grandeur.

The Pine and the Sea
Species: *Pinus parviflora*
(Japanese Five Needle Pine)
Age of tree: 90 years old
Spread: 65 cm
Container: Hexagonal sandy clay pot
Designer: Li Ming
Introduction: This cliff-hanging style pine has its long trunks extending well beneath the brim of the pot, as if overlooking a sea below. The dead branches at the top contrast artistically with the green layers of leaves, showing the great vitality of the pine. The long branches progress downward, displaying a tremendous momentum.

Dancing Fairy Maidens
Species: *Sageretia theezans*
(Chinese Bird Plum)
Age of tree: 60 years old
Height of tree: 85 cm
Container: Rectangular glazed
pottery tray
Designer: Wu Chengfa
Introduction: This is
interlocking-root style. The
Chinese Bird Plum trees have
developed from stumps. With
their exposed interlocking roots,
the trees are like dancing fairy
maidens.

Cloud, Branches, and Shade
Species: *Bougainvillea* spectabilis
(Brazil Bougainvillea)
Age of tree: 35 years old
Height of tree: 120 cm
Container: Rectangular sandy
clay tray
Designer: Wu Chengfa
Introduction: This weeping
style penjing has been wired
and pruned into a tree with
willow-shaped foliage. The
vivid interplay of sparseness
and denseness produces an
extremely vivid picture.

Autumn Wind
Species: *Fraxinus chinensis* (Chinese Ash)
Age of tree: 50 years old
Height of tree: 100 cm
Container: Rectangular stone tray
Designer: Wu Chengfa
Introduction: This windswept style penjing features an old tree, deprived of all leaves in the strong autumn wind blowing continuously from one direction.

93

Tree in Peak
Species: *Sageretia theezans*
(Chinese Bird Plum)
Age of tree: 25 years old
Type of rock: Ying Rock
Length of container: 45 cm
Container: Glazed pottery pot
Designer: Wu Chengfa
Introduction: Root-in-rock
style. This Chinese Bird Plum's
roots progress along the cracks
in the rock, with the foliage
high above as if overlooking
a valley. Balance is well kept
between the tree, the rock, and
the tray.

Species: *Ficus microcarpa*
(Chinese Banyan)
Age of tree: 20 years old
Type of rock: Taihu rock
Height of tree: 60 cm
Container: Container made of
wood blocks
Designer: Han Xuenian
Introduction: This root-in-rock
style specimen features a typical
Chinese Banyan in the wild.
The container made of wood
blocks is unique, yet natural
looking.

95

A Pine in Lingnan
Species: *Pinus massoniana*
(Chinese Red Pine)
Age of tree: 40 years old
Height of tree: 135 cm
Container: Rectangular glazed
pottery tray
Designer: Han Xuenian
Introduction: Literati style. With
sparse foliage, the two trunks
with the same root contrast well
in size. Simply structured, the
work is thought-provoking.

96

A Pine atop Mountain Ridge
Species: *Pinus parviflora*
(Japanese Five Needle Pine)
Age of tree: 35 years old
Height of tree: 70 cm
Container: Hexagonal sandy
clay pot
Designer: Zhao Qingquan
Introduction: This literati style
Japanese Five Needle Pine has
a well-structured, simple shape,
but with much individuality.
The trunk progresses toward
left well beyond the limits of
the container. This specimen
portrays what Huang Tingjian,
a well-known poet in the Song
dynasty, said in one of his poems
to the effect that the sound of
wind in pines atop a mountain
ridge can be heard miles away.

Cowboy in a Forest
Species: *Sageretia theezans* (Chinese Hackberry)
Age of tree: 50 years old
Height of tree: 150 cm
Container: Rectangular marble tray
Designer: Wu Chengfa
Introduction: This forest penjing consists of two multi-trunk Chinese Hackberry trees with interlocking roots, with the one on the right as the dominant tree. The composition shows a clear sense of variation in trunk thickness, height, and density of the branches. The cowboy on a bull's back adds greatly to the vivid picture.

Sparse Forest in Spring
Species: *Sageretia theezans* (Chinese Bird Plum)
Age of (main) tree: 40 years old
Type of rock: Turtle Shell Rock
Length of container: 100 cm
Container: Oval marble tray
Designer: Meng Guangling
Introduction: The forest-style water and land penjing has its dominant part on the left. The trees in the front are taller, while those at the back are in a descending order in terms of height. The part of the creek closer to the viewer also has a wider water surface. The whole composition has a clear sense of sparseness and denseness as well as balance between emptiness and substance.

Forest Penjing

With two or more trees in a pot or tray, forest penjing represents the changing landscape of a forest in nature: dense or sparse forests, old or young forests, forests in autumn or winter, forests seen at different distances. It also features forests in different ecological environments with different characteristics: in a plain, in a valley, in the mountains, in a marsh, on a beach, along a stream, on a highland.

Different from other types of penjing, forest penjing feature groups of trees which compete with and complement one another at the same time, revealing a beauty of unity and change.

In traditional Chinese painting there are numerous classics which feature groups of trees in the wild. They serve as a good source for penjing beginners to learn how trees can be arranged in a forest penjing. Of course, natural landscapes can be another source for them (see page 98, top).

Source Trees

Trees with dense foliage and the shape of a large tree are among the best source trees for a forest penjing. In most forest penjing specimens, the trees are all the same species, and they can be straight, slanting, or with curves. When two or more species are chosen, one of them must dominate the design and the unity of them will be very important.

One of the trees to be planted in a tray should be the tallest with the largest trunk. It is almost impossible to arrange trees of similar sizes for a penjing (see page 98, bottom).

The trees for a penjing should, by and large, have a similar shape, and they can be straight, slanting, or with curves. However, it is important that variety is added to your design. For example, it lends to your work much liveliness and naturalness to have one or two slanting or curving trunks when the dominant tree is straight and upright (see page 101).

A forest penjing is always viewed as a whole and, therefore, too much work on an individual tree at the cost of others, which actually undermines the appeal of your design. At the same time, it is advised that a tree with many unconventional features should not be selected, for it is hard to match it with others.

Layout

A good starting point for beginners to learn about the layout of a forest penjing is to distinguish between dense and sparse forests and near- and far-view forests. In a forest penjing, if the number of trees can be figured out at a glance, it is sparse, otherwise it is dense. If you are portraying a forest as if you are close to it, pay attention to dominance and subordination, and put larger trees in the front. On the other hand, the trees in a far-view penjing do not vary much in size, and the focus should be the overall outline and space arrangement.

All forest penjing with three or more trees comprise a planting of an odd number of trees in a tray. Whatever the number, three of them serve as the leading trees, with the main or number one tree as the tallest and strongest one.

Viewed from the direct front, the main tree is never at the center or near the edge of the tray, but somewhere at the one-third point to the right or left edge of it. Viewed from the side, it is near the central axis, but not on it. The number two tree is often placed on the other side at the one-third point, while the number three tree is near the number one, but not parallel to it. In practice this basic layout is followed, but variations are always added. However, the silhouette of the group and that of the foliage of the trees as a whole are always scalene triangles.

These basic rules of penjing apply to a forest with more trees. For example, a five-tree forest can be designed by adding one tree at the two sides, somewhere near the number one and number two trees. When a seven-tree forest is to be created, two trees can be planted at each side.

With more trees added, a three-tree forest is expanded into three groups of trees, with the basic rules observed: any three trees in the group form a scalene triangle, rather than a straight line, with a curvy silhouette of the foliage.

The trees in a forest penjing should be well-spaced to allow light to penetrate into the forest and air to circulate.

Layout for three-tree combination (I).

Layout for three-tree combination (II).

Layout for five-tree combination.

Layout for seven-tree combination.

Pines in *The Mustard Seed Garden Painting Manual* (I).

Pines in *The Mustard Seed Garden Painting Manual* (II).

Pines in *The Mustard Seed Garden Painting Manual* (III).

Broad-leaved trees in *The Mustard Seed Garden Painting Manual* (I).

Broad-leaved trees in *The Mustard Seed Garden Painting Manual* (II).

Broad-leaved trees in *The Mustard Seed Garden Painting Manual* (III).

Peaceful Sparse Forest
Species: *Acer palmatum* (Japanese Maple)
Age of (main) tree: 25 years old
Height of tree: 80 cm
Container: Rectangular glazed pottery tray
Designer: Zhao Qingquan
Introduction: Sense of dominance and subordination. The forest penjing consists of several Japanese Maple trees. The main tree is the largest and tallest one, which is placed at the one-third point to the left edge of the container. It is well balanced with other trees to form a gorgeous forest.

100

Water Running on Rocks
Species: *Pinus parviflora*
(Japanese Five Needle Pine)
Age of (main) tree: 35 years old
Length of container: 70 cm
Container: Round marble tray
Designer: Meng Guangling
Introduction: You can see variety
in tree shapes. This water and
land specimen was created to
echo Tang dynasty poet Wang
Wei's poetic image with a round
marble tray. The components
are artistically arranged to
highlight the towering pines,
with the help of rustic rocks.
The water running on the
rocks creates a strong dynamic
quality. The whole composition
is well structured with a sense
of firmness and gentleness and
a balance between dynamic and
static features.

101

Rainy Day in Foreign Land
Type of rock: Sandstone
Length of container: 80 cm
Container: Round marble tray
Designer: Gao Liliang
Introduction: Plant accents in landscape penjing. This near-view landscape features tall and rugged peaks. The main peak and the accompanying peaks are handled with a clear sense of heaviness and lightness. The small trees and grasses display a gentle quality amid imposing grandeur. The shoreline is geologically varied and with a balance between what to conceal and what to reveal. The gray sandstone is best exploited to represent the emotions of a traveler on a rainy day in a foreign land.

Landscape Penjing

As a unique Chinese creation, landscape penjing is depicted using rocks as the major source material, with scenes of high mountains, lofty hills, valleys, rivers and lakes in shallow water pots. They are often referred to as three-dimensional Chinese landscape paintings.

As mentioned earlier in Chapter I, rocks, tray, complementary plants and other adornments must be prepared before rocks are cut and the layout is designed.

Layout

A layout of a landscape penjing should be made with the comprehensive consideration of all source materials in hand according to the central theme, including its style, the position of the highest peak of the mountains, and arrangements of the rocks, water surface, complementary plants and other adornments.

As the focus of the landscape, the position of the highest peak of the mountains is all the more important and should be first determined. It is usually at the one-third point to the right or left edge of the tray, near but not on the horizontal axis of the tray. Rocks can then be placed around the peak to form a complete scene of a hill. The rocks should be arranged to coordinate with the peak to form a unified whole. The peaks should avoid similarities in height and shape, and the layout should achieve a balance between denseness and sparseness, as well as emptiness and substance.

The Mustard Seed Garden Painting Manual, a well-known textbook for the acquisition of Chinese painting skills for generations of students in China, serves as an excellent reference for landscape penjing designers.

Single-peak style features the entirety of a single domineering mountain peak in a tray. The rock is always off the center of the tray.

Off-center style consists of two groups of rocks at the two sides of a tray, with the main group larger and more domineering than the other, forming a contrasting unity.

Opening-and-closing style is a three-set combination of rocks, with the tallest and second tallest

Natural hills (Zhangjiajie, Hunan Province).

Natural water and hills (Lijiang River, Guilin, Guangxi Province).

Landscape scene in *The Mustard Seed Garden Painting Manual.*

Markings on rock in *The Mustard Seed Garden Painting Manual.*

Landscape in *The Mustard Seed Garden Painting Manual.*

groups at the two sides of the tray and the other one in between and behind them. Viewed above it, the three groups form a scalene triangle.

Sprinkle style consists of three or more groups of rocks which appear to be scattered in a container. While one of them is the largest group, the rest are subordinate to it. The groups can be spaced in various ways.

Multi-peak style comprises several lofty peaks, which vary in their importance in the composition, featuring competing peaks or ranges of hills.

Complementary Plants

Accessory plants, grass, and moss add much liveliness to a penjing scene. However, designers need to know where in the tray they grow best before they are added. Herbaceous

Rivers and the Lake
Type of rock: Ying Rock
Length of container: 90 cm
Container: Rectangular marble tray
Designer: Xu Fulin
Introduction: Single-peak style. With the top of the single peak at the one-third point to the left edge of the tray, the penjing reveals the imposing manner of a complete landscape.

Spring Rain
Type of rock: Ying Rock
Length of container: 100 cm
Container: Rectangular marble tray
Designer: Xu Fulin
Introduction: Off-center style. The work consists of two visible parts, with the major part on the right and the accompanying one on the left. The larger and the smaller hills contrast artistically to contribute to the harmony of the composition as a whole.

Peaks in Clear Day
Type of rock: Ying Rock
Length of container: 100 cm
Container: Oval marble tray
Designer: Xu Fulin
Introduction: Opening-and-closing style. The work consists of three visible parts, with two in the front of the tray and the lowest far in the back. The dominant is on the right. The design highlights the depth of the scene.

Spring in Southern China
Type of rock: Ying Rock
Length of container: 90 cm
Container: Oval marble tray
Designer: Xu Fulin
Introduction: Sprinkle style. The three groups of rocks are scattered over the tray. While one of them dominates the design, others are incorporated as accents with good spacing.

The River and the Peaks
Type of rock: Ying Rock
Length of container: 120 cm
Container: Oval marble tray
Designer: Xu Fulin
Introduction: Multi-peak style. This penjing features competing multiple peaks separated by water, with a clear sense of dominance and subordination.

plants, together with the soil attached to their roots, are often planted in cracks in the rocks, and they are regularly watered to ensure their healthy growth. For woody plants, holes in rocks are needed to accommodate their roots and should be filled with soil when they are planted (see page 102).

Miniatures

Small as they are, miniatures are significant for landscape penjing in that they help to develop a specific theme, enhance the lyrical mood and the profound image of a scene, or to establish a sense of proportion.

It is important to keep right proportions between your miniatures and the rocks and trees and between your miniatures. Pottery or stone miniatures can be glued onto a rock or the tray with cement; metal accessories are often affixed with water-proof adhesives. Small structures like bridges and boats usually stand by themselves.

With the miniatures in place, a landscape penjing is complete.

Miniatures in landscape penjing.

Water and Land Penjing

Water and land penjing combines the former two types of penjing to feature "richer" scenes of water, land, trees and rocks, by using their techniques. If you have mastered the techniques for designing tree penjing and landscape penjing, you will find a water and land penjing is not as hard as you had imagined. Even knowing how to create one of them helps, too.

Source materials

Before you can actually begin with a tentative layout of a water and land penjing, it is always worth preparing the materials that will be needed—trees, rocks, pot, and miniatures—and working on them by pruning the trees and cutting the rocks.

Layout

A tentative layout is the key to any successful composition and worth the time and effort needed. Without a conception in advance, any effort would lead to waste or loss of the materials chosen.

Start your composition by tentatively grouping the trees, rocks, pot, and miniatures together and exploring an overall sense of harmony and structural coherence, before you actually start to work on them.

An idealized water and land landscape is created using the trees as the main artistic medium, while rocks and miniatures are incorporated as accents. Among the trees, one of them must dominate the composition while others are positioned to relate to it. All rocks and miniatures are not equally important, either, and the main ones should be easily recognized.

Generally, trees should be located before soil is added. This is followed by rocks. Of course, trees and rocks can also be placed alternatively. When several trees are to be planted in a container, follow the guidelines for forest penjing, but with positions of rocks and water in mind.

When rocks are added, those for shorelines, which divide the land mass and water, need to be placed before others are placed first on land and then in water. As for sizes of rocks, consider the need for perspective. As a general guideline, place taller pieces toward the front and lower ones toward the back. However, rather than looking like a flight of steps, they should vary in height as well as in size so that they are a natural and dynamic group. At the same time, the layout of rocks should coordinate with the trees.

Shorelines have to bend in a variety of ways, but it is important that they are adequately short to viewers in the direct front of the penjing. In a word, frequent

Natural "water and land" scene (North Carolina, US).

observation of rocks in natural landscapes helps with the layout of rocks in penjing creation.

Rocks can be placed on land and in water, adding variety to the landform and water area. This is done sometimes to make up for the unsatisfactory base of a tree. Rocks on land need to be placed so that they are well related to shorelines, trees, and the land mass, and those in water should vary in size and be well spaced.

As the composition of a water and land penjing is more complex than that of a tree or landscape penjing, the whole layout can be divided into several smaller penjing, where they each have their own dominant features and accents. However, it is essential that they form a harmonious and coherent whole.

Water and land penjing can be roughly classified into the following categories:

Shoreline style. With a rock line dividing land and water areas, shoreline

A stream in a water and land penjing. This is a detail of *Sparse Forest in Spring* (see page 98 for a more detailed introduction to it).

"Water and land" scene in *The Mustard Seed Garden Painting Manual*.

105

Bridge, River and Farm House
Species: *Buxus sinica* (Chinese Box)
Type of rock: Turtle Shell Rock
Container: Oval marble tray
Length of container: 150 cm
Designer: Zhao Qingquan
Introduction: With techniques from several water and land penjing styles, the combination style specimen features a landscape with a farm house and a stone bridge. With the right land mass as the dominant component, the composition shows balance between the land and the water with variations in tree and rock arrangement.

style portrays a forest scene along the shoreline. Trees are planted on the land mass, with rocks as accents, and small rocks and boats are incorporated in the water. The shorelines have to be geologically and structurally diverse (see page 108).

Island style. This style usually features a piece of land that is surrounded by water. A penjing with two or three islands are rare but can be seen sometimes. It can be an island with water on all sides, but it can also be a peninsula joined to the pot rim on one side. The island needs to be irregular in shape, with a diverse shoreline and varied land. Rocks can be placed in water as coral reefs. In a penjing with two or three islands, the islands should vary in size and the dominant one is easily recognized. This style is often used to represent small islands in a river, lake or sea (see page 110).

Creek style. This style consists of two pieces of land separated by a narrow stretch of water (creek). The asymmetrical

land parts often incorporate tree and rocks and vary in height. The creek needs to be geologically and structurally diverse to look natural, and rocks are often included. Creek style penjing feature creeks and streams in forests. It is the best category that shows the depth of a natural landscape (see page 109).

River or lake style. This styles features two pieces of land separated by a broad stretch of water (river or lake), sometimes with lower rocks at the back to

Natural shorelines (Jinbian Stream, Zhangjiajie, Hunan Province).

Shorelines in *The Mustard Seed Garden Painting Manual*.

A shoreline in the water and land penjing entitled *Fisherman* (see page 80 for more details to it).

Interspersed rocks in the wild (Shenshi Mountain, Jeminay County, Xinjiang).

Rocks in *The Mustard Seed Garden Painting Manual* (I).

Interspersed rocks in soil of water and land penjing.

Interspersed rocks in water of a water and land penjing.

Rocks in *The Mustard Seed Garden Painting Manual* (II).

Quiet Bay
Species: *Sageretia theezans* (Chinese Bird Plum)
Age of (main) tree: 35 years old
Type of rock: Turtle Shell Rock
Container: Rectangular marble tray
Length of container: 150 cm
Designer: Zheng Yongtai
Introduction: This is shoreline style. In this forest scene at a riverside, the land and the water are separated by a line of rocks. On the land are several Chinese Bird Plum trees with interlocking roots, while a couple of rocks are interspersed in water. The curvy shoreline is geologically varied.

(facing page)

Quiet Forest
Species: *Ulmus parvifolia* (Chinese Elm)
Type of rock: Turtle Shell Rock
Container: Round marble tray
Length of container: 70 cm
Designer: Zhao Qingquan
Introduction: This is a creek style penjing. The land part on the right dominates the composition with a bigger land mass and the largest tree. The creek in between shows great depth with its varied structure and interspersed rocks of various sizes. The specimen features a creek in a forest in a natural landscape.

Poetic Image of Ni Yunlin
Species: *Lagerstroe indica* (Crape myrtle) and *Punica granatum* (Pomegranate)
Type of rock: Turtle Shell Rock
Container: Round marble tray
Length of container: 70 cm
Designer: Zhao Qingquan
Introduction: This river or lake style penjing represents the poetic image of Ni Yunlin, a well-known painter in the Yuan dynasty. The two forests are separated by a wide river. With two hills further back, gentle slopes, and varied shorelines, the specimen portrays a beautiful lake landscape.

Drinking Horse in Spring
Species: *Serissa foetita* (Snowrose)
Age of (main) tree: 30 years old
Type of rock: Turtle Shell Rock
Container: Oval marble tray
Length of container: 80 cm
Designer: Zhao Qingquan
Introduction: This island style penjing specimen features a small island with water on three sides. With the rise and fall of the terrain, the varied shoreline and the rock in the water, the penjing produces an extremely vivid picture.

110

represent distant mountains. With trees, rocks, and soil, the land part is often with forest penjing trees, mild slopes and diverse but gentle shorelines. The water part is much wider than that in creek style, with bridges or boats as miniatures. This style portrays landscapes of rivers or lakes (see facing page, bottom).

Combination style. Real landscapes in nature are not necessarily so neatly defined and simple that merely one basic style above can well represent them. The combination style is a blend of two or three styles above to capture more complex and natural landscapes (see facing page, top).

Potting

As the major artistic medium of water and land penjing, trees should be trained and trimmed as the first step of the process. All trees for water and land penjing need to be trained and pruned in an alternative container for a period for a preliminary shape. When they are potted in the pot selected, they need to be carefully pruned again according to your tentative layout. Refer to Chapter Three for a detailed introduction to the pruning techniques.

Start your composition by tentatively putting the trees in the container. Once you have decided upon a layout, proceed with planting the trees.

Mark on the container surface with a pencil the positions where trees are to be planted and shorelines are to be located as accurately as possible. Then remove the trees and rocks and start planting the trees.

While adding soil, work it around the root mass with a bamboo rod so that there are no air pockets. Continue to add soil until the whole of the root is covered with soil. It is important that soil should be placed within the limit of the land mass so that rocks are easily cemented. The gaps

can be filled when rocks are attached to each other.

Affixing Rocks

When trees are in position, affix the rocks to appear along the shoreline and in the water to the container surface with waterproof cement.

Before the affixing work, mark the positions where rocks are to be placed on the container surface with a pencil and, if necessary, number them in case they are mistakenly located.

It is desirable to choose rapid hardening cement and add water pigment color to it to make it go with the rocks for visual effect.

Rock surfaces need to be clean and dry. Apply a full, even coat of silicone cement on the bottom side of the rock and carefully place it in the desired position. Make sure that all rocks are well attached to the container bottom and to each other so that no gaps have been left between them for water leakage. Then use a wet brush to brush away small cement stains that are left behind.

When all rocks for shorelines and slopes have been set in place, check again to see if there are gaps left that allow water to go through to the land mass, which will be bad to the growth of trees and plants as well as the aesthetic effect of the water part. So if you find a leak, fix it quickly by applying a little more cement.

When soft rocks are used to create shorelines, the side attaching to the soil needs to be coated with a thick layer of cement to prevent water from seeping into the soil.

Landscaping

Different from tree penjing, water and land penjing requires careful landscaping to create the overall design of the composition.

When rocks are all cemented, more

soil can be worked in to link shorelines and the land mass and to form, with the help of interspersed rocks, an undulating landform. Landforms vary from scene to scene, but generally shoreline style and river or lake style specimens are with gentler land surfaces than creek and island penjing.

The rocks are not "scattered" over the land mass, but "planted" in the soil in the manner that a tree is planted. To observe interspersed rocks jutting above the loose sand in the wild is one of the best ways to learn the techniques.

The last step in landscaping is to spread a thin layer of fine "decorative soil" on the surface of the land mass, on which mosses and lichens can be added.

Miniatures

The placement of miniatures should be appropriate. Structures such as boats and arch bridges can be affixed onto the tray, and stone slab bridges are often simply placed over a river. The best places for pavilions, terraces, houses, figurines, and animals are rocky slopes and interspersed rocks on the landmass, where stone slabs are sometimes buried for miniatures.

Places for miniatures need to be leveled before they are placed. Pottery and stone structures are usually cemented on a rock or pot surface with silicon cement mixed with 107 glue. Metal accessories are often affixed with water-proof adhesives. Small structures like bridges and boats usually stand by themselves.

Mosses and Lichens

Mosses and lichens play a very important part in the overall composition of a water and land penjing by linking the tree, rock, and soil as a whole. While helping to safeguard against soil erosion, it is often used to feature grassland or groups of

A tree being potted.

Layout of trees.

Creating a shoreline.

Marks being made for rock.

Cement being applied to bottom of rock.

Rock placed with force.

Cement residue being removed.

A figurine in a penjing.

A boat in a penjing.

Adding mosses.

Small grasses and flowers add liveliness to a scene.

Quiet Forest
Species: *Acer buergerianum* (Trident Maple)
Type of rock: Turtle Shell Rock
Age of (main) tree: 15 years old
Container: Oval marble tray
Length of container: 130 cm
Designer: Zhao Qingquan
Introduction: This is a newly created water and land penjing in forest style. The primary tree dominates the design, while other trees are incorporated as accents around it with a clear sense of sparseness and denseness.

bushes. It is important that one type of moss dominate the design, while other types may act as accents to show variety.

Mosses and lichens are found in places with enough humidity and can be dug out with a small scraper. Make sure you have removed the weeds before they are planted.

Use a sprayer to wet the soil before patches of mosses or lichenes are placed on it. Be sure to press them slightly so that they are well attached to the soil.

When you feel satisfied with your work, you may want to add some small grasses and flowers to it for liveliness.

The last step is to fine-tune all details and make any adjustments you deem necessary. First, re-evaluate the overall composition in relation to your desired effects, to see if more work is needed to perfect it. Then prune the trees for the last time, bearing in mind that the trees are well related to each other and to the rocks so that the entire landscape appears a complete entity. Some minor wiring work may be needed at this time. This is followed by a thorough cleaning of the trees, rocks, and the container using a brush. The last step is to spray water over all the components of the composition. It is important that they should not be too wet, because a second watering is needed after the cement is fully set up to soak the land mass and the water part needs to be filled with an appropriate amount of water. Thus a water and land penjing specimen, by and large, is finished.

With timely care and maintenance, your specimen will be as natural and attractive as it can be in about two years.

CHAPTER FIVE
DISPLAYING TECHNIQUES

Aesthetic rules are often followed to in a penjing to allow a viewer to see all the important features of the penjing from the most advantageous position.

Displaying penjing for viewers differs from placing it for care and maintenance. While the former focuses on the aesthetic effects of the work, the latter stresses the living habits of the plants as well as convenience in maintenance work.

Displaying penjing at different places requires different designs: indoor display differs from outdoor display, and displays in public places differ from those in house yards.

Specifically, the environment, the background, the size, and height of the space, and the category, shape, size, and color of the plant, the pot or tray, and the frame are important factors to be considered. The relationship between the viewer and the penjing is also crucial for a display.

Size Classifications

While there is no universally acknowledged ranges of size for penjing specimen in China, the following classification is often employed in national exhibition catalogs.

Tree Penjing
The height of a tree in a tree penjing is the distance between the root and the tallest part of the tree, but that in a cliff-hanging style, cascade style or lying style is measure by the distance from the root to the furthermost leaf on the longest branch.

    Super-large: over 120 cm
    Large: 90-120 cm
    Medium-sized: 50-90 cm
    Small: 16-50 cm

Landscape Penjing and Water and Land Penjing
These two kinds of penjing are classified by the length of the tray.

    Super-large: over 120 cm
    Large: 90-120 cm
    Medium-sized: 50-90 cm
    Small: 16-50 cm

Miniature Penjing
When the height of the tree in a tree penjing or length of the tray for a landscape penjing or water and land penjing is under 16 cm, it is called a miniature penjing.

Penjing specimens with different sizes are often displayed in different manners.

Basic Guidelines

Environment
Like living species in the wild, potted plants die without sunlight and air. Penjing specimens, therefore, need to be placed in a well-lit and airy environment. As most rooms are not as sunny as an outdoor space and the air in it does not circulate as well, which influence the process of photosynthesis of plants, it is important to learn how long a specific plant can survive when living indoors. Leaving a penjing in a house for too long a time will inevitably lead to damages to it and, therefore, it needs to be returned to an outdoor environment from time to time. When new leaves are growing, the plant needs to live outdoors.

Backgrounds
Like Chinese landscape paintings, penjing needs a neat and clean background, the design behind the work, to highlight their artistic effects. The background for

Living in Mountains
Species: *Ulmus parvifolia* (Chinese Elm)
Age of (main) tree: 45 years old
Type of rock: Turtle Shell Rock
Container: Natural-looking pottery container
Length of container: 165 cm
Collector: Penjing Museum of Yangzhou
Introduction: Chinese landscape paintings can serve as the background to show the poetic image of the penjing work. This was a demo work created in 2011 by an artist from Penjing Museum of Yangzhou for visitors from Bonsai Clubs International. It features a natural landscape with two Chinese Elm trees, with the help of the small trees and grasses.

Spring in the House
Species: *Pinus thunbergii* (Japanese Black Pine), *Juniperus chinensis var. sargentii* (Sargent's Chinese Juniper), *Ilex canariensis* (Small-leaved Holly), *Acer buergerianum* (Trident Maple), *Fraxinus chinensis* (Chinese Ash), *Podocarpus macrophyllus var. maki* (Yew Plum), *Berberis thunbergii* (Japanese Barberry) and *Parthenocissus tricuspidata* (Virginia Creeper)
Height of frame: 85 cm
Designer: Li Yunlong
Introduction: A miniature penjing grouping on a *bogu* frame. The miniature penjing involves several species with different styles, which are potted in different containers, featuring variety in unity.

a penjing needs to be plain and quiet in color so as to leave the focus of the whole on the artistic work itself. Sometimes, penjing specimens are placed in a natural environment, being part of a larger landscape. Most penjing are designed to allow the viewer to appreciate it in the defined front and, therefore, its background is often at the back, facing the viewer.

Height

Generally, a penjing is placed at the height where its surface of the container is slightly lower than the viewer's eye level. This allows the viewer to appreciate the design of the water, land, slopes, and other ornamental sets. Sitting the penjing so low that the viewer appears to be hovering in the sky above it or so high that the viewer appears to be looking up at the tree from beneath the ground is a typical mistake, which misleads the viewer. However, cliff-hanging penjing specimens should be placed on floor frames, so that they are at the height of the viewer's eyes.

Space

Penjing specimens should be displayed in a space of appropriate size. While a space too large makes your specimens smaller, a space too small makes the view uneasy.

A medium-sized or small penjing is often placed indoors on a tabletop to allow closer appreciation; a large one is displayed for viewers both in front of it and at a reasonable distance; and miniature penjing on *bogu* frames usually form a group.

This is a combination of penjing specimens in an outdoor display area in Penjing Museum of Yangzhou. With the viewer in the front, the gray wall serves as the background for a pictorial effect of the display. The windows on the walls at the sides help with the air circulation.

The Cloud and the Pine
Species: *Pinus parviflora* (Japanese Five Needle Pine) and *Rhododendron simsii* (Azalea)
Type of rock: Turtle Shell Rock
Age of (main) tree: 150 years old
Length of container: 6 m
Container: Rectanglar cement tray
Collector: Penjing Museum of Yangzhou
Introduction: Display of large specimens allows both near- and far-view appreciation. With two Japanese Five Needle Pines of 150 years old and natural Turtle Shell Rocks in a super large container of 6 m long and 4 m wide, the specimen which is the largest water and land penjing in Yangzhou, portrays the natural pines in wind and clouds.

116

Frames

It is said in Chinese penjing tradition that "the frame comes only after the tree or landscape and the pot." This means that the frame is no less important than the pot in a penjing display. It is often not viewed by penjing artists as a pedestal, but rather as a viewing platform to highlight the beauty of your penjing tree or landscape by adding to the overall balance and ambiance of your penjing in content as well as structure. Therefore, the frame is itself a work of art.

Frames can be used for indoor and outdoor purposes.

Outdoor Frame
All outdoor frames stand on the ground. They are often made of stone, wood, or cement so that they are firm and durable. Some outdoor frames are built by laying bricks or stones.

Indoor Frame
Indoor frames can be placed on the floor or on the table,

An outdoor wood frame.

An outdoor stone frame.

An outdoor stone frame.

and they are often made of wood or bamboo.

Floor frames are usually about 80 cm in height and they are for large or medium-sized water and land penjing specimens. Table frames, usually small and low, are made of red sandalwood or other hardwood.

Table frames can be single or combined. Single frames are often lower, but their tops need to be larger than the pot to be placed on. Combined frames are often four-piece sets for square or round pots or trays; they can match a variety of penjing specimens.

Indoor floor frames.

A rectangular indoor table frame.

A round indoor table frame.

A root-shaped indoor table frame.

An indoor frame set.

A square indoor frame set.

An arched indoor frame set.

117

Display at home. This was an arrangement in Zhang Yi Penjing Demonstration held in Suzhou, China, in October 2005.

An indoor exhibition area at Penjing Museum of Yangzhou.

Penjing and Chinese landscape painting. The specimen entitled *Rainy Day in Foreign Land* (see page 102 for details) and the background painting is carefully orchestrated to complement each other with a great sense of emptiness and substance, showcasing the nature of penjing as a tri-dimensional painting.

Indoor Display

Penjing specimens can be displayed indoors at home, at exhibition, or in public places. Many specimens are often placed indoors temporarily as they need outdoor living conditions for healthy growth.

Display at Home

Specimens placed indoors on a frame on a tabletop are often medium-sized or small ones. Some indoor penjing are displayed on individual floor frames. Miniature specimens traditionally go with decorated *bogu* frames and several of them are often placed together.

Considerations of indoor penjing placement include the size, color, and position, which should match the indoor environment to allow the viewer to appreciate your design as part of the home decor. It is often placed near or along a wall, which serves as its background, to allow space for human activities. Calligraphic scrolls hanging on the wall often go well with it, but they should never overlap.

Display at Exhibition

All specimens, other than super-large ones, can be placed at exhibition halls. While matching the design of the hall itself, each specimen should be the focus. The guiding principle is that the background serves the penjing, not vice versa. The background is usually white or light gray. Chinese landscape paintings can serve as the background to show the poetry of the penjing work.

The halls need to be well-lit and airy, but not too big. Large ones are often divided into smaller spaces with boards.

Water and land penjing are generally placed on an exhibition booth of appropriate height, on which penjing frames are placed. Floor frames are used when booths are not available.

Variations should be kept by alternation of different types of penjing specimens. It is advisable that one specimen should not be placed in front of another.

Display in Public Hall

Penjing can be placed in halls for public use for decorating purposes. Super-large specimens are usually not preferred, as they are not easy to be changed. Penjing in halls in a garden should not only go along with the halls but the outside surroundings.

Outdoor Display

Penjing can be displayed outdoors in a penjing garden, a yard in house, or a public place.

While all types of penjing specimens can be displayed outdoors, the space where they are placed should not be too large.

As outdoor displaying is often over a long period, living conditions such as sunlight, air, and weather should be taken into consideration and measures be taken to protect the plants in summer and winter. The arrangements should allow easy care and maintenance, and species with different light-loving natures are suggested to be separated. Local climate conditions and living habits of the plants should be considered when measures are taken to deal with the summer heat and the winter cold.

The background of a penjing for outdoor display should also be as simple as possible. A wall of a building can be used as the background or a special structure can be designed. The best background walls or structures often have windows or holes that allow air and light for the living plants. When penjing specimens have to be placed without a background structure, it is suggested that each penjing specimen be well spaced with a proper distance from the one behind it to avoid disorderly presentation.

While large penjing specimens can be displayed as individual items, medium-sized or smaller ones are often placed in combination, with varying heights and density.

Outdoor placement as a long-term display shares important features with display at exhibitions, and it should be designed to stress the penjing work rather than the background. Penjing gardens are artistic representations of penjing specimens, and the designs should last well in outdoor environments.

In large penjing gardens similar specimens are often placed in an exhibition area for better viewing effects and easier maintenance, but with variations in design, size, and structure, which is usually pursued in smaller gardens by alternative arrangements of different types of work.

The large space of a penjing garden is often divided with boards or walls into smaller exhibition areas, where varying sizes of penjing are displayed, with one or two large dominant specimens. While large ones are designed to show their individuality, smaller ones form an organic group as a unity.

Displays in a yard in a house and in a public place are part of the decoration of the environment. They should match the place as a whole, and be convenient for appreciation and maintenance. As for super-large specimens, they need to be displayed at a central or important position.

An indoor display in a hall at a landscape garden. The pine penjing entitled *Soughing of Wind in Pines* (see page 44 for a more detailed introduction) is placed before a rockery to form a larger landscape.

This is an outdoor display area at Penjing Museum of Yangzhou.

Outdoor display at Penjing Museum of Yangzhou.

Outdoor display at Shanghai Botanical Garden.

CHAPTER SIX
CARE AND MAINTENANCE

As live plants, penjing trees need not only good living conditions to grow but regular watering, fertilizing, pruning, repotting, and treatment of pests and diseases. The purpose of this is to keep their healthy and pleasing artistic shape. More care is needed when your penjing tree is a rare aged species.

The techniques required for the tree penjing are essential for all types of specimens. With a variety of species, such as pines and junipers, foliage penjing, and flower- and fruit-effect plants, tree penjing enthusiasts should follow important techniques and design guidelines, to help their specimens grow healthily and to maintain their designed shapes.

The care and maintenance of landscape penjing often focuses on the small plants, including moss, that grow on rocks. The small trees are often cared for by following the necessary maintenance procedures for miniature penjing.

While the care and maintenance of water and land penjing is similar to that of tree penjing, more patience and care are necessary because the soil in the pot or tray is often shallower. To control the size and shape of the trees so that they are proportion to the surrounding is not always easy, but needs to be maintained.

Placement

Most penjing species need an outdoor environment where they receive maximum light and air for good budding and healthy, compact growth. Days of life indoors or under the shade of a tree or porch will result in yellowing leaves or even fall of leaves due to lack of sunshine, air and natural moisture. This is especially the case when they are in their growing season. Shallow-rooted water and land penjing has less soil in its tray and strong sunlight should be avoided in the summer, but it should be placed in a sunny place in the house in winter.

Plants can be either light-loving species or shade-loving species in their native habitat. For example, species such as pines and junipers prefer full sun while others, such as azalea, snowrose and littleleaf box, need much less sunny places. Effective shading measures must be taken in hot summer to protect these specimens from direct sunlight.

Penjing plants vary from species to species in their preference to temperature and measures are maybe required according to the climate in which they are kept. Cold-resistant species can survive the winter outdoors, but the pot can be wrapped up with thermal insulation materials or placed underground, if needed, to avoid the root being frozen as the temperature falls. Species that cannot survive the outdoor cold in the winter should be placed indoors or in a greenhouse to help them live through the season.

All shallow-rooted penjing and miniature penjing should be placed indoors in the winter and measures taken in the summer to avoid exposure to direct sunlight.

(facing page)

Penjing specimens are placed in well-lit and well ventilated location. This is a maintenance area at the Penjing Museum of Yangzhou.

Outdoor penjing in the winter. Specimens with cold-resistant species usually winter outdoors, but long periods of low temperature may be damaging. This is an outdoor display area at the Penjing Museum of Yangzhou.

Watering

Correct watering practices are an essential part of the care for the health of a penjing. While allowing the soil to dry out will kill a penjing, as the tree lives in limited quantity of soil which cannot hold enough water, overwatering will lead to overgrowth of the branches and leaves. At the same time, overwatering creates a permanently wet environment in which the root system lacks oxygen; this reduces the ability of the compost to absorb air, causing the roots to suffocate and even leading to death of the tree.

A guiding principle for watering penjing is that "it requires water only when the top centimeter of the compost has started to dry out and, when it does, it needs a thorough soaking." However, in practice this depends upon a variety of factors:

Type of species. Different trees have different water requirements. Generally speaking, species with broad leaves require more water than those with narrow waxy leaves, because broader leaves help water to evaporate. Pines and junipers, for instance, prefer an environment with less moisture.

Season and weather. Trees have different water requirements in different seasons and weather conditions. Trees tend to need watering every day or every other day on fine and cloudless days in the spring and autumn, while they need to be watered twice a day—in the morning and evening—in the summer, with additional watering at noon and spraying of water on the floor and on their leaves when there is a drought or dry-hot wind. In the cold winter, trees are in the state of dormancy and they can be watered once every several days.

The air is often heavy with moisture when it is cloudy, which reduces evaporation

Watering a penjing.

Applying diluted organic solution with a sprayer.

of water from the leaves of the tree and the soil in the pot, and less water is required. Watering is normally not needed when it is raining.

Drainage of soil. Trees growing in soil with excellent drainage require more water than those in soil with average drainage.

Finally, a water and land penjing without adequate drainage holes will have water collected. So it is important to prevent water-logging in the bottom.

Trees should be checked routinely, so their water requirements can be observed: they can be watered when the leaves seem to be withering or when the soil surface starts to dry and change to a lighter color.

Water your tree thoroughly so water can be seen running out of the drainage holes at the base of the pot. Otherwise it still lacks water though the soil sufrace is wet.

Use a hose fitted with a spray gun to water your tree, but do not spray on the soil directly, which will disturb it.

For water and land penjing and landscape penjing, a sprayer is needed, when necessary, to water the moss on the tree and rocks.

Fertilizing

A tree planted in the ground is able to extend its root system in search of

nutrients; however, a tree planted in a penjing pot is unable to do so. For a penjing tree to continue to grow healthily, the soil it grows in must have its nutritional content repeatedly replenished. However, over-fertilizing will lead to overly large trees with overly large leaves from excess nitrogen, which disturbs their proportion to their surroundings. At the same time, if the nitrogen content of the soil becomes too high it will "burn" the roots.

Soluble organic fertilizers are mixed with water and applied to the whole of the soil surface, while organic compound fertilizers are placed on top of the surface of the soil.

Fertilizers are different in the major, minor, and trace elements that they contain. Use the recommended amount of the right type of fertilizer.

The major plant nutrients required if plants are to grow satisfactorily include nitrogen (N), phosphorous (P), and potassium (K). Plants for leaf growth primarily use nitrogen; phosphorous in the form of phosphates is mainly used for flower and fruit production, and potassium for root and stem growth. This means different species needs different amounts of each element at different growth stage. For example, foliage plants (grown for their leaves) need more nitrogen than flower-

Applying organic solution with a scoop.

5. The best time for fertilizing is when the soil in the pot is drying out, but watering is needed immediately afterwards.

6. Fertilizing is not suggested when it is raining, but it can be done before it rains.

7. It is advisable not to fertilize your penjing when it is too hot or when the tree is in the state of dormancy or at the early stage of its flowering and fruiting phase.

8. Reduce the amount and concentration of fertilizer for a tree that grows too fast or is not growing well due to poor health.

Pinching a Japanese Five Needle Pine.

Granular fertilizer for penjing.

Pinching and Pruning

When the tree in a penjing grows, it must be pinched and/or pruned on a regular basis to keep its diminutive shape and artistic beauty. By regular pruning, the tree grows healthily and its pleasing outline is kept.

Apical pinching. With this technique, new apical growth within the vigorous areas of the tree is partially or completely removed before it extends, so that vigor is displaced more evenly amongst the branches of the tree.

Bud-pinching. Bud-pinching refers to eliminating undesirable buds that emerge on a branch of a pine and juniper before they become active, to allow other branches to better grow and to maintain the pleasing outline of the design. Species such as Chinese Elm, Chinese Bird Plum and Chinese Firethorn need to be frequently observed for new buds that should be pinched. About 1/2 of the buds on a pine and juniper should be removed before the needles come out.

Leaf pruning. The display season for foliage penjing trees and plants is when they grow new leaves. The new growth of a Japanese Maple and pomegranate is red, and old leaves are often picked out to allow

Pruning a Chinese Elm.

young leaves to sprout several times a year for its color. The leaves of Chinese Elm and maidenhair tree are also removed for fresher leaves and postponement of their defoliation.

Branch pruning. This refers to the removal of branches to shape the penjing into the desired form; from time to time, long branches are cut short and excess branches are trimmed. Every year new growth brings with it unwanted branches that need to be cut back and altered so that the style of your tree is maintained. Common types of unwanted branches that you may want to redirect or cut off include dead, overlapping, parallel, symmetrical, and trunk crossing branches.

and fruit-effect plants (grown for their flowers and fruits), which require more phosphorus.

Do's and Don'ts of Fertilizing

1. Organic fertilizers such as bean or rape-seed cakes need to be thoroughly decomposed before they are placed on the soil.

2. Soluble organic fertilizers should be mixed with enough water before it is applied to the soil.

3. Newly repotted penjing should not be fertilized to avoid burning new roots.

4. The leaves should be avoided when applying fertilizer.

Repotting

As time passes, the growing roots of a penjing tree occupy the limited space in a pot and, with less nutrition, the soil structure deteriorates, becoming less permeable for air, fertilizers or water to allow the tree to grow. Plants that grow in penjing pots, therefore, must be repotted from time to time, to change the condition of drainage and soil for the healthy growth of the tree.

More often than not it is the soil rather than the pot that is changed. Of course, a larger pot can be used instead if necessary.

Fast growing species with more branches and leaves and large root systems need to be repotted more frequently, while trees that grow slower and need less fertilizer require less frequent repotting. However, repotting is necessary for any penjing tree when the soil structure deteriorates and the tree is root-bound in its pot. Generally speaking, most plants need to be repotted in two to four years. However, some penjing designed for flowers and fruits are often repotted every year.

Gently lift the tree with its roots and soil out of the pot. Remove around 1/2 of the old soil, cut off the dead roots and disentangle any long roots that will need to be trimmed back. For well-developed, densely packed root balls, it may also be necessary that excess circling roots be trimmed back before the tree is placed in the fresh soil.

The best time to repot a tree is right at the end of its dormant period in spring or late autumn, just as it is about to start back into growth.

Removing half the old soil.

Repotting with new soil.

Spraying agricultural chemical on leaves.

Roots attacked by disease.

Pests and Diseases

As living trees, penjing are susceptible to certain pests and diseases, and preventive treatments and therapies are no different from those for similar species in the ground. The only difference is that potted trees may be less competitive in their ability of resistance to attacks of pests and diseases due to their limited space, which requires regular inspection and immediate action when pests or diseases appear.

Agricultural chemicals pollute the environment and cause ecological contamination, so it is advisable to use less of them. When they have to be used, a low-toxin pesticide needs to be selected and the suggested directions be strictly followed.

Common Diseases

Root diseases. As penjing grows in years, bacterium- or fungus-related root rots and root knots may develop. It is therefore necessary to sterilize the soil and to avoid overwatering.

Branch diseases. Stem rot and canker are the commonly seen branch diseases, with symptoms that include the appearance of small areas of dead tissue on bark or at the heart, or spots on twigs. To deal with them, Bordeaux mixture can be sprayed on boughs and twigs or lime sulfur mixture applied.

Leaf diseases. The leaf diseases common with penjing plants include leaf spot, leaf yellowing, and powdery mildew, which cause yellow or black pots on leaves, curly dwarfs, and withering leaves. Leaves with blemishes can be removed or Bordeaux mixture can be sprayed on the leaves; leaf yellowing can be treated with 0.1-0.2% solution of ferric sulfate on the leaves; and powdery mildew with lime sulfur solution.

Common Pests

Aphids. They are small soft insects with varying colors, are among the most destructive insect pests on trees. Dense colonies of aphids may be found along stems or buds or on the underside of a leaf.

A trunk attacked by disease.

Leaves attacked by disease.

They feed themselves through sucking mouthparts called stylets on the sap of phloem vessels in plants, causing leaves and stems to become distorted, which may lead to the fall of leaves or death of the tree.

Natural predators such as lady beetles and lacewing flies, which feed on aphids, may provide adequate control. They can also be controlled by using small brushes. Pesticide controls have to be conducted when non-chemical measures are not effective enough.

Scale insects. They are common parasites of penjing trees, feeding on sap drawn from stems, leaves or fruits. They vary dramatically in their appearance, but most scale species have a waxy covering. Severe infestations of scale insects can result in yellowing of the infected part, retardation of the tree's growth, and even the death of the tree.

For minor infestations of trees, scale insects can be rubbed off using a brush or bamboo sticker. Removal and disposal of infected branch or stem may be effective, along with pesticides that are registered for use in controlling scale insects.

Red spiders. They are classed as a type of mite. While they are small in size, their fast development rate and high egg production can lead to extremely rapid increases in mite populations, especially in hot and dry weather. Damaged areas typically appear marked with many small, grayish yellow light flecks. Following severe infestations, leaves become discolored and then drop prematurely, which may result in the death of the tree.

Penjing trees need to be checked for red spiders from time to time especially when it is hot by placing a piece of white paper under the tree and padding the tree gently. When they are seen on the paper, chemical measures should be taken before damage becomes extensive.

Adult lace bugs. They are about 3.5 mm long and dark brown in color. They are often found on the undersides of leaves and feed on the sap with their needle-like mouthparts into leaf tissue, which causes white spots on the surface and yellow rusty blotch of their excreta and feces on the other side of the leaves. Heavy feeding can cause early leaf drop, which result in distorted growth of the tree. They are often most damaging in the summer.

Lace bugs can often be effectively controlled by timely removal of the fallen leaves and weeds in the area. Chemical measures can also be taken when necessary.

Longhorn beetles (longhorns). They often bite the bark of a tree trunk or the base of a primary branch and lay eggs there. The larvae feed under the bark in the living tissue of the tree for a period of time and then bear into the wood as far as the root. Repeated attacks lead to dieback of the tree crown, yellowing of leaves and branches and, eventually, the death of the tree.

Flowering quince leaves attacked by aphids.

Flowering quince leaves attacked by scale insects.

Sargent's Chinese Juniper attacked by red spiders.

A Chinese Flowering Crabapple leaf attacked by lace bugs.

A flowering quince branch attacked by longhorn beetles.

Adult longhorn beetles on tree trunks and branches can be manually killed in June and July. To kill the larvae, chemical solution can be injected into the holes where they live and immediately block these holes with clay, or metal wires can be directed into the holes.

The guidelines and techniques introduced in previous sections apply to all categories of trees and plants. However, penjing artists need to familiarize themselves with the living habits of the particular trees that they are to train, so that they know how to take proper care of them.

While many trees are trained for penjing purposes, thirty-two of them are introduced in this section. This also serves as a reference for those who grow other trees or plants of the same category.

Coniferous Species

Buddhist Pine

With narrow, elliptical leaves that are stiff in texture and spirally crowded together, the evergreen Buddhist Pine makes penjing with great artistic value. Shortleaf Podocarpus is even more treasured by artists, but you have to wait for years to have a mature tree.

A nice indoor penjing tree, this conifer loves partial shade and moisture. Shading is necessary in the hottest weeks of the summer. When it is placed in a outdoor location, it

Dense Shade in Summer
Species: *Podocarpus macrophyllus* (Buddhist Pine)
Age of tree: 120 years old
Height of tree: 105 cm
Container: Rectanglar sandy clay tray
Collector: Penjing Museum of Yangzhou
Introduction: This decorative Buddhist Pine penjing was created in the traditional style. The branches and leaves have been wired into layers of "cloud."

Buddhist Pine

needs to be moved to an indoor site in places where temperature falls below 0 °C.

Buddhist Pine handles shade and moisture extremely well, so keep compost damp, but not saturated. You may want to spray water on leaves periodically in the summer for better leaf color.

The conifer is usually fed two or three times in the spring with a thoroughly decomposed and diluted liquid cake fertilizer. Reduce fertilizing in the autumn to avoid bud development, which always lead to cold damage.

Pruning can be performed all year round to keep its shape by removing water sprouts or damaged branches.

It is repotted every three or four years in March or April before new growth appears. Remove about half of the old soil before it is repotted in loose, fertile soil with humus.

Buddhist Pine penjing has trouble with bagworm moths, scale insects, and red spider mites, and it can be infected with sooty mould and leaf spot.

Chinese Cypress
The bud green leaves of Chinese Cypress

turn reddish brown in autumn. The whorled roots indicate how firmly the tree is standing in the soil.

The cypress loves full sun and warmth and moist locations. It cannot tolerate cold, so it is desirable to place it in a site where temperature is above 5 °C.

Chinese Cypress loves damp sites, and soil needs to be kept moist. Water it immediately when the soil becomes dry. It cannot tolerate drought, and can be planted in a water pot.

The conifer is usually fed monthly in growing months with thoroughly decomposed and diluted liquid cake fertilizer or any other organic fertilizer.

Chinese Cypress grows fast, and unwanted buds can be pinched off in a short time. Redundant young shoots can be removed now and then to keep shape.

With a fast-growing root system, Chinese Cypress needs to be repotted every three years, usually in February or March. Remove a proper amount of old soil and redundant roots before it is repotted in slightly alkaline or neutral soil.

A healthy tree, Chinese Cypress seldom has trouble with pests and diseases.

Early Spring
Species: *Cupressus duclouxian* (Chinese Cypress)
Age of tree: 40 years old
Height of tree: 115 cm
Container: Rectanglar stone tray
Designer: Wu Chengfa
Introduction: The extremely large trunk and the whorled roots of the cypress indicate how firmly the tree is standing in the soil. The bud green leaves of the Chinese Cypress in spring turn reddish brown in autumn.

Chinese Cypress

Creek Water
Species: *Pseudolarix amabilis* (Golden Larch)
Type of rock: Stalagmite rock
Length of container: 60 cm
Container: Round marble tray
Designer: Zhao Qingquan
Introduction: The water and land penjing represents a forest with a dozen of Golden Larch seedlings. The dominant and subordinate parts are separated by a creek, in which the water is so clear that you can see the bottom.

Golden Larch

Golden Larch

With graceful shapes and golden yellow leaves in autumn, Golden Larch trees make wonderful penjing specimens.

Golden Larch loves light and can tolerate mild cold, and it needs to be located in a warm environment with full sun and good moisture. It is desirable to move it to an indoor place in winter where temperature never drops to below zero. Shading measures are required in the hottest summer weeks.

It does not tolerate drought, so keep pot soil damp. Water it as soon as the soil becomes dry, but water logging is damaging to it.

Feed it monthly with a thin liquid cake fertilizer during the growing season, but not in hottest weeks of the summer.

A fast-growing tree, unwanted buds can be removed now and then when new growth starts, to keep its pleasing shape; redundant shoots developing later can also be cut out whenever they seem to be unnecessary.

It is repotted every three or four years in February or March in the early spring. Remove a proper amount of old soil in root

fertilizing should be avoided. Feed it once or twice with a thoroughly decomposed and diluted liquid cake fertilizer during growing season every year.

Japanese Black Pine must be significantly pruned to keep its pleasing shape and beautiful small needles by pinching new growth. Bud pinching should be conducted in March or April to remove half of the stronger ones of the buds on shoots that developed the previous winter.

When your pine grows too fast, all new needles and the majority of old needles can be removed at their base in June, leaving two or three lines of old ones untouched. New buds will develop at the base about one month later, and then remove once again the unwanted ones. The new growth will be smaller as expected due to the shortened growing period. This is the process of "de-candling."

Japanese Black Pine grows well in any type of soil, but it prefers sub-acid or neutral soil with good drainage. It is generally repotted every three to five years during February to March.

Japanese Black Pine has trouble with rust disease, leaf cast, curve twig disease, and Eastern Pine Gall Rust. It can be attacked by aphids, scale insects, red spider mites, and knot-horn moths.

Green Needles
Species: *Pinus thunbergii* (Japanese Black Pine)
Age of tree: 45 years old
Height of tree: 90 cm
Container: Round sandy clay pot
Collector: Penjing Museum of Yangzhou
Introduction: Japanese Black Pine is a popular penjing tree. The specimen features a pine in a hilly country, which usually has a curved trunk with vigorous branches and evergreen leaves.

Japanese Black Pine

mass damaged roots and some of the old roots before it is repotted in loose, fertile sub-acid sandy soil. It is important for its healthy growth to use a deep enough pot.

Golden Larch has trouble with damping-off disease, stem rot, pine-leaf-cast and psychidaes.

Japanese Black Pine
Japanese Black Pines, one of the common evergreen penjing species, have upright trunks and dark green foliage with thick, hard needles or candles.

It tolerates cold and drought extremely well, and can be placed in a location with full sun and good air circulation. However, those in small or shallow pots should be protected from over exposure to sunshine during the hottest weeks of the summer.

Japanese Black Pine can withstand drought, so over-watering and excess of water in pot should be avoided. Reduction of watering in growing period will lead to thicker trunk and branches and shorter needles, promoting its artistic value.

The pine withstands poor soil, so over-

Japanese Cork-bark Black Pine

Like Japanese Black Pine, the Japanese Cork-bark Black Pine is a conifer with firm needles or candles. The main difference is that it has corks on its bark, as the name suggest, making a wonderful penjing with great artistic value.

It tolerates mild cold and loves warm and moist locations, and it can be placed in a position with full sun and good air circulation. However, those in small or shallow pots should be protected from the cold of the winter by moving them indoors.

Japanese Cork-bark Black Pine prefers drier soil, so excess of water in pot should be avoided. Reduction of watering when fresh needles are growing will lead to thicker trunk and branches and shorter needles, promoting its artistic value.

The pine does not require much of fertilizer, and feed it once or twice with a thoroughly decomposed and diluted liquid cake fertilizer during growing season.

Japanese Cork-bark Black Pine needs to be pruned to keep its pleasing shape by pinching off new growth. Bud pinching should be conducted in March or April to remove one-thirds or half of the stronger ones of the buds on shoots that developed the previous winter. The rule of thumb is that the higher the buds the more of them

Protective Covering of Scales
Species: *Pinus thunbergii var. corticosa* (Japanese Cork-bark Black Pine)
Age of tree: 30 years old
Height of tree: 45 cm
Container: Rectanglar sandy clay tray
Designer: Zhao Qingquan
Introduction: The charcoal-shaped bark of the Japanese Cork-bark Black Pine looks like the unique scales of a dragon.

Japanese Cork-bark Black Pine

should be de-candled, and leaving along those weak buds.

Japanese Cork-bark Black Pine loves loose, fertile soil with good drainage. It is generally repotted every three or five years, in the period from February to March.

Like Japanese Black Pine, Japanese Cork-bark Black Pine has trouble with rust disease, leaf cast, curve twig disease, and Eastern Pine Gall Rust. It can be attacked by aphids, scale insects, red spider mites, and knot-horn moths.

Japanese Five Needle Pine

A valuable classic tree for penjing, the Japanese Five Needle Pine, or Japanese White Pine, has a strikingly vigorous trunk and a dense, conical crown with short needles.

The tree needs full sun and air but a condition with moisture. In the hot summer, it should be placed in a shaded and cool environment, avoiding direct sunlight. In the cold winter it overwinters indoors, but with a temperature under 10°C for its dormancy. When it is dry, water can be

sprayed on the ground to keep the humidity in the air.

One of the most important things to remember about the Japanese Five Needle Pine is that the soil must be dry and has good drainage. However, a dry soil condition for a long period of time is also damaging to it.

A conifer tree, it needs less frequent fertilizing and a smaller dosage. A mixture of fertilizer cake and with a large amount of water can be fed 2-3 times in spring when it is growing. While the same fertilizer is often used with a greater concentration in autumn, it is not to be fertilized since October.

Pinching is the most important method to control the shape of a Five Needle Pine. During March to April, you will need to pinch off any new shoots to about one-third to half their length before the needles come out, which of course would depend on the number, density and length of the new growth as well as the design. The redundant new shoots should be removed, but wound dressings may be necessary.

Japanese Five Needle Pine prefers sub-acid soil with good drainage. Repotting should be performed every three to four years. Typically, this is done in February or March. However, you can also repot in late fall, once the temperature has dropped.

The pests that attack the conifer tree include scale insects, aphids, and red spiders. It can be infected with rust disease and root rot.

Green Cloud
Species: *Pinus parviflora* (Japanese Five Needle Pine)
Age of tree: 70 years old
Height of tree: 65 cm
Container: Rectanglar sandy clay tray
Designer: Zhao Qingquan
Introduction: The foliage of the Japanese Five Needle Pine has been trained into cloud-shaped clusters. With a curved trunk and layers in the foliage, the penjing features a pine in the high mountains.

Japanese Five Needle Pine

location without further measures taken.

The juniper loves moist environments, so keep the soil damp, but not saturated, in spring and summer when it is in growing season. In dry days, spray water on its leaves and the ground where it is placed, to promote leaf growth.

Thoroughly decomposed and diluted liquid cake fertilizer or any other organic fertilizer can be applied monthly during growing season.

Branch pruning can be performed to keep shape in spring before new leaves develop. Pinching is done periodically in its growing season to encourage development of lateral branches for denser foliage.

The juniper is repotted every two or three years in February or March in early spring before new growth appears. Remove about one-third to half of old soil and prune redundant roots before it is repotted in soil with good air permeability.

The pest to be controlled is the red spider mite, and it can be infected with rust disease.

Sargent's Chinese Juniper

This evergreen is a popular penjing due to its dense foliage with thin needles, curvy trunk and branches, and simple but elegant shape. It can be displayed all year round.

It needs to be placed in a moist location with full sun. Partial shading is required in the hottest weeks of the summer, and an indoor location without further protective measures will suffice over winter .

Sargent's Chinese Juniper needs to be watered plentifully, but without excess water in pot. Frequent spraying on leaves helps it grow better and maintain its beautiful leaves.

A thin thoroughly decomposed liquid cake fertilizer or any other organic fertilizer needs to be applied twice or three times

Vicissitudes of Life
Species: *Sabina procumbens* (Creeping Juniper)
Age of tree: 35 years old
Height of tree: 55 cm
Container: Hexagonal sandy clay pot
Designer: Zhao Qingquan
Introduction: The Creeping Juniper penjing has a curved trunk and extending foliage. It is not a large tree, but it seems that it has gone through all the vicissitudes of life.

Creeping Juniper

Procumbent Juniper

With dense foliage, curvy branches, and dark green leaves, the evergreen Procumbent Juniper is at it best as a penjing when fresh leaves are produced in spring.

Procumbent Juniper is light-loving and can tolerate shade, and it needs to be placed in a partially sheltered environment with good humidity. Shading is necessary in the hottest weeks of the summer, but the site needs to be well ventilated. Being cold-resistant, it is often placed in indoor in the period from March to May. A thoroughly decomposed organic fertilizer can be used as base fertilizer.

Branch pruning can be performed to keep shape of its dense foliage in spring and summer before new leaves develop. Use fingers rather than shears to remove tops of new shoots. Large branches need to be pruned, if needed, when it is in dormant season.

It is repotted every three or four years in February or March in early spring or in late autumn. Remove about one-third to half of old soil and prune the roots before it is repotted in loose, fertile neutral soil.

Sargent's Chinese Juniper may have great trouble with red spider mites, and it can be attacked by rust disease.

The Aged Pine
Species: *Juniperus chinensis var. sargentii* (Sargent's Chinese Juniper)
Age of tree: 20 years old
Height of tree: 75 cm
Container: Natural-looking pottery tray
Designer: Zhao Qingquan
Introduction: A literati penjing, this tree has a long, thin bare trunk and a crown with drooping branches covering one-third of the tree. It is not old in age, but it looks like a tree in an ancient Chinese painting.

Sargent's Chinese Juniper

Taiwan Juniper

One of the popular penjing trees in China, this evergreen juniper has a rustic structure. Its trunk or branches are ideal material on which *sheli* or *shari* can be created.

Taiwan Juniper loves full sun or partially shaded but well-ventilated location. It can tolerate the heat of the summer as well as the cold of the winter.

The juniper does not handle drought well, and excess water in pot is damaging to its roots. It is important to place it in a location with good humidity.

A thin thoroughly decomposed liquid cake fertilizer or any other organic fertilizer needs to be applied twice, both in spring and autumn. A thoroughly decomposed organic fertilizer can be used as base fertilizer in autumn.

A fast-growing tree, Taiwan Juniper penjing requires a hard pruning in spring before new growth starts. Pinching can conducted any time when needed to keep shape.

Taiwan Juniper is repotted every two or three years in February or March in early spring before new growth appears. It grows well in loose, fertile sub-acid soil.

The pests to be controlled are the long-horned beetles, and red spider mites.

Lofty and Unyielding Character
Species: *Juniperus formosana* (Taiwan Juniper)
Age of tree: 80 years old
Height of tree: 120 cm
Container: Rectanglar marble tray
Designer: Wu Chengfa
Introduction: With the long bare trunk and the sparse branches and leaves, this literati penjing aims to portray the lofty and unyielding character of Chinese literati and their preference to a simple, rustic life.

Taiwan Juniper

early new growth, which have negative impact on budding in the coming year.

A shallow-rooted plant without a tap root system, Azalea has thin fibrous roots. It therefore requires light fertilizing. Feed it every two weeks in growing months. No fertilization schedule is required after autumn months.

Azalea should be pruned when it is at state of dormancy. Long branches are cut back and redundant shoots are removed to keep its pleasing shape and to allow air and light to penetrate into foliage. In addition, flower stalks need to be pinched off when blooming is over, to reduce the unnecessary consumption of nutrition.

Azalea penjing trees need to be repotted every two or three years when the flowering months end. It can also be done in early spring or late autumn. Remove about one-third of old soil in root mass and prune redundant roots before it is repotted in loose, fertile acid soil with good drainage.

Azalea trees have trouble with pests such as bagworm moths and lace bugs, and its diseases include leaf spot and rust disease.

Deciduous Species

Azalea

One of the top ten best-loved flowering shrubs in China, Azalea produces stunning blooms and beautiful leaves. It is available in a variety of category, with different flowering periods.

Azalea should be placed in a well-ventilated location, where it is always kept away from direct exposure to sunlight, especially in the hottest weeks of the summer season. It can be kept in a shade or a place where it is able to get filtered sunlight. Azaleas vary in their tolerance of frost and cold: while some can withstand moderate cold, most of them need to be placed indoor in winter.

Water your Azalea penjing regularly to ensure the soil maintains moisture. It requires more water in flowering season, so the soil needs to be soaked frequently and, if needed, water can be sprayed on the leaves. Reduce watering in autumn to avoid

Stunning Flowers
Species: *Rhododendron simsii* (Azalea)
Age of tree: 50 years old
Height of tree: 70 cm
Container: Oval sandy clay tray
Designer: Rui Xinhua
Introduction: Azalea is trained mainly for its flowers, although its leaves can be attractive, too. This aged but vigorous tree with large branches produces stunning flowers.

Azalea

Brazil Bougainvillea

With flower-like bracts, Brazil Bougainvillea can be a very showy plant.

Brazil Bougainvillea loves full sun and moisture and should always be placed in a location with good sunlight. Being a warm weather plant, they must be moved to greenhouses in winter in those cold areas.

The bougainvillea requires more water than other vines, so it is important to keep pot soil moist. However, during the period from July to August, water it until the soil dries out, a schedule which promotes development of more flowers. In winter, when it is placed indoors, watering is needed only when the soil begins to dry, but a thorough soaking of the soil is necessary when it does need water.

As a plant with long flowering season, Brazil Bougainvillea needs to be fertilized frequently. While applying enough base fertilizer when repotting, a liquid cake fertilizer is required once a week in its growing season.

A fast-growing vine, it needs to be pinched and pruned timely to keep desired shape. Bud pinching also encourages ramification for more flowers. Pruning is usually conducted in spring or summer, but never after mid August.

Brazil Bougainvillea needs to be repotted annually. While it grows well in most soil types, loose, fertile compost with good drainage is desirable.

Aphids, slug moths, and scale insects attack the bougainvillea, and it has trouble with leaf spot (see page 2).

Brazil Bougainvillea

Chinese Ash

With small branches and tiny leaves, Chinese Ash has dense foliage in summer and autumn. It also looks vigorous even when the curvy branches are free of leaves in winter.

It loves full sun and moisture, so place it in a well-ventilated, well-lit location. It can tolerate the heat of summer and the cold of winter extremely well.

Chinese Ash needs to be watered adequately, but excess water in the pot should be avoided.

Thin fertilizers are needed frequently.

Old Tree Full of Life
Species: *Fraxinus chinensis* (Chinese Ash)
Age of tree: 80 years old
Height of tree: 75 cm
Container: Oval sandy clay tray
Designer: Wu Chengfa
Introduction: This Chinese Ash has been trained from an earlier stump. The sense of dominance and subordination is highlighted by the two broken trunks. While the tree is old, it produces a vigorous crown.

Chinese Ash

Feed it every two weeks in growth season.

A fast-growing plant, Chinese Ash responds well to pruning. Pinching can be performed now and then, and unwanted branches can be removed and branches that overgrow can be cut back. In its dormancy, larger branches are pruned, leaving small shoots untouched.

It needs to be repotted every two or three years in February or March. Remove about half of old soil in root mass and prune old roots before it is repotted in loose, fertile neutral or sub-acid soil with good drainage and air permeability.

Although a healthy plant, Chinese Ash may be attacked by yellows due to alkaline soil and pests such as flower thrips and scale insects.

Chinese Banyan

This evergreen is a popular penjing due to its dark green foliage and ancient-looking twisted root. It can be displayed all year round.

Chinese Banyan prefers warm and moist location with full sun and good air circulation. Partial shading may be needed in the summer and it requires an indoor environment when temperature falls below 5°C.

While it can tolerate mild drought, it loves moist compost and needs to be watered plentifully in its growing season.

Frequent feeding with thoroughly decomposed liquid cake fertilizer will suffice for its growth, but a base fertilizing is desirable in winter.

Chinese Banyan grows fast and often needs pruning. Dead, broken, and unpleasing branches can be removed in spring before the growth starts. Water sprout branches can be removed to keep shape from time to time.

Chinese Banyan is repotted every two or three years, usually in April or May.

The banyan has trouble with cottony cushion scales and thrips. To deal with them, infected leaves can be removed before pesticide is applied.

Region of Rivers
Species: *Ficus microcarpa* (Chinese Banyan)
Age of tree: 30 years old
Container: Oval sandy clay tray
Length of container: 120 cm
Designer: Zheng Yongtai
Introduction: This shoreline style single-tree penjing is created by using a large, old Chinese Banyan and Ying Rocks to represent a landscape in quiet and peaceful Southern China. The banyan has simple but natural foliage. The horizontal branch links the tree with the water below, adding to the imposing manner and dynamic nature of the old tree. The easy life of the villagers can be felt from the old man and the boy, who are sharing the history of the village under the tree.

Chinese Banyan

Overlooking the Valley
Species: *Sageretia theezans* (Chinese Bird Plum)
Age of tree: 40 years old
Spread: 45 cm
Container: Round porcelain pot
Designer: Xu Ronglin
Introduction: The Chinese Bird Plum penjing has an aged rough trunk, roots and upwardly diagonal branches with small green leaves. With its foliage out of the container, the penjing features an old tree on a cliff overlooking the valley below.

Chinese Bird Plum

Chinese Bird Plum

Chinese Bird Plum has dense branches, as well as rustic trunks and roots. Its small leaves, when young, are stunning dark green in spring, but it is even more gorgeous when it is without leaves in winter.

It is usually placed in a well-lit location with good air circulation. Shading is necessary in the hottest weeks of the summer.

Keep pot soil moist. When it is hot or dry, check soil regularly to see if it dries out.

Thin cake fertilizer is desirable in growing months for better growth.

Pruning is often performed to keep shape when autumn comes to an end, by thinning dense part of the foliage and removing unpleasing branches and water sprout branches.

It is repotted every two or three years in early spring before new growth appears. The Bird Plum grows well in any type of soil.

Chinese Bird Plum trees have trouble with long-horned beetles and scale insects.

Chinese Elm

The Chinese Elm tree has small glossy green leaves, corky bark and a pleasing shape. The best view of a Chinese Elm penjing is when it is producing new shoots in early spring.

Although they can tolerate an environment without sunlight, it is a light-loving plant and needs to be placed in a warm and moist condition where there is full light with good air permeability.

It should be watered regularly. Water it twice a day in hot summer days—in the morning and evening. However, it needs less watering during autumn months and even less during winter when it is without leaves.

Feed it twice a month with diluted organic fertilizer during growth season. In winter a base fertilizer will suffice.

Branches need to be pruned in the period from April to May in spring and in autumn when the leaves have fallen. To maintain its shape, unnecessary new growth can be pinched from time to time.

Chinese Elm penjing trees need to be repotted every two or three years, in early spring before the growing season starts or in late autumn. They grow well in almost any type of soil.

Chinese Elm penjing trees can experience problems with leaf beetles, scale insects, or red spider mites.

Chinese Elm

Graceful Bearing
Species: *Ulmus parvifolia* (Chinese Elm)
Age of tree: 60 years old
Height of tree: 58 cm
Container: Oval glazed pottery tray
Collector: Penjing Museum of Yangzhou
Introduction: The Chinese Elm tree has small glossy green leaves, corky bark, and a pleasing shape. The best view of a Chinese Elm penjing is when it is producing new shoots in early spring. While the trunk leans slightly toward the right and a large branch extends out, the composition is well balanced by the exposed strong root on the left.

139

Chinese Firethorn

Chinese Firethorns are known for their beautiful white flowers in early summer and bright red berries in autumn.

The Firethorn prefers warm, moist places with full sun. While it can tolerate moderate cold, shading is needed in the hottest weeks in summer.

Generally speaking, it is important to keep pot soil moist, but it requires more water in flowering and fruiting months. Less frequent watering is needed in the autumn and winter.

Feed twice a month in periods of growth and flowering and fruiting with a high-phosphorous and high-potassium liquid organic fertilizer to promote flowering and fruiting. A base fertilizer can be applied in winter.

Chinese Firethorn branches often grows in a disorder way, so a hard pruning is needed every year when the leaves have dropped. Water sprouts can be cut back in fruiting season according to the distribution of fruiting branches.

It needs to be repotted every two or three years. Remove about half of old soil in root mass and prune redundant roots before it is repotted in loose, fertile soil in the pot.

Pests that attack the Firethorn include lace bugs, aphids, and scale insects.

Autumn
Species: *Pyracantha fortuneana* (Chinese Firethorn)
Age of tree: 25 years old
Height of tree: 40 cm
Container: Rectanglar glazed pottery tray
Designer: Zhao Qingquan
Introduction: Chinese Firethorn penjing is kept for its flowers as well its fruits. With a curvy trunk and extending branches, the Firethorn is even more gorgeous when its fruits turn red in autumn. The tree has been train for 25 years from a seedling.

Chinese Firethorn

Chinese Flowering Crabapple

This graceful tree produces magnificent fragrant flowers during the spring months, followed by small, red fruits that look like miniature apples.

The flowering crabapple loves full sun and good air circulation, so shading is not needed in summer. A hardy plant, it is also cold-resistant.

This particular tree needs adequate watering during growth months, so keep soil in pot moist, but too much water should be avoided. Frequent watering is needed in hot summer days but less is required in winter when they are without leaves (see page 10).

Chinese Flowering Crabapple

Chinese Hackberry

Chinese Hackberry has a beautiful upright trunk and graceful shape. It produces dense green foliage in spring and summer, which turns yellowish in autumn. The bare branches in winter can also be stunning.

A light-loving tree, it prefers a location with full sun and good air circulation. Shading is only desirable in the hottest weeks of the summer. It can withstand mild cold in winter.

The hackberry handles drought fairly well, so over-watering is damaging to it. While soil needs to be moist in spring and summer, it seldom needs watering in autumn and winter months.

Thin liquid cake fertilizers are periodically needed in growing season, and a base fertilizing can be conducted when winter approaches.

The Chinese Hackberry grows fast. Cut back new growth to two or three leaves when it is 6-8 cm in length. A hard pruning is needed in winter to keep shape.

It needs to be repotted every two or three years in early spring before new growth appears or late autumn. While repotting it, old and weak roots should be removed to allow new growth. It grows well in any type of soil.

Chinese Hackberry has trouble with powdery mildew and pests such as red spider mites, long-horned beetles, aphids, jumping plant louses, and cottony cushion scales.

Straight Trees with Horizontal Branches
Species: *Sageretia theezans* (Chinese Hackberry)
Age of tree: 60 years old
Height of tree: 90 cm
Container: Rectanglar glazed pottery tray
Designer: Wu Chengfa
Introduction: The several separated trunks of one Chinese Hackberry tree with various heights form a stunning forest landscape.

Chinese Hackberry

The flowering crabapple needs to be fed more frequently and with a larger dosage, but a solution containing proper nitrogen, phosphorous and potassium is required.

It is repotted annually or biennially, usually in February or March prior to bud burst or in late autumn. While it grows well in any type of soil, loose and fertile compost mix is desirable. While repotting, root and branch pruning is often done at the same time.

A fast-growing tree, it needs hard pruning when it is at its state of dormancy, and redundant new growth can be removed when it is growing in spring. After the flowering period, long branches can be cut back to allow side shoots to encourage flowers in the coming year.

The flowering crabapple has some problems with aphids, scale insects, lace bugs, slug moths, and long-horned beetles. It can be attacked by brown blotch.

Chinese Plum

A traditional Chinese penjing tree, Chinese Plum is well-known for its shape, colors, and graceful bearing.

Chinese Plum needs adequate sunlight and good air circulation, so place your penjing where it will get enough sunlight. It can withstand average low temperatures in winter.

It is important to keep pot soil moist, but not saturated, and water it only when pot soil becomes dry. Reduce watering in May and June as these two months are crucial for the differentiation of flower bud. Water it only when the leaves are about to wither, to promote development of more buds. Return to your normal schedule in July.

Feed it once or twice before buds develop in May and again in early August. In autumn, fertilize it twice or three times. Bone meal or thoroughly decomposed cake fertilizer can be applied at the bottom of the container when repotting it.

As the plum flowers on new shoots, old branches are often cut back after the flowering season to two or three sprouts for denser flowers in the coming year. Unwanted branches are removed to help shape.

It needs to be repotted annually or biennially, usually after the flowering period. Remove about half of old soil in root mass and prune dead roots and cut back long old roots before it is repotted in loose, fertile soil with good air permeability.

Pests that attack Chinese Plum are aphids and red spider mites, and the plant has trouble with leaf-curl, anthracnose, and sooty mould.

Chinese Plum

Showcasing Flowers
Species: *Prunus mume* (Chinese Plum)
Age of tree: 40 years old
Height of tree: 65 cm
Container: Hexagonal glazed pottery pot
Collector: Penjing Museum of Yangzhou
Introduction: As a traditional Chinese ornamental species, the Chinese Plum is considered a symbol of Chinese national spirit and loved by the literati. This specimen is pruned into a slanting shape with sparse boughs and twigs. Every year when the flowering season ends, the branches are cut back to promote new growth for flowers in the coming year.

Chinese Quince

Chinese Quince has robust branches, which produce bright red flowers in early spring and decorative fruits in autumn.

It needs to be placed in a location with full sun and good air circulation. Partial shade in midsummer is desirable in hot areas, and it can tolerate average low temperatures in winter.

While it grows well by keeping the soil moist, more water is needed when it is in flowering season. It is important to water frequently in hot summer days to avoid yellowing leaves due to lack of water.

Feed it frequently with thin liquid fertilizer in growth months and with a base fertilizer in winter.

It needs to be repotted every two or three years, usually at the dormant state after the flowering season or in autumn. Chinese Quince grows well in loose, fertilize subacid or neutral soil with good drainage.

As a general rule, cut back branches which have flowered, to encourage ramification for more flowers in the coming year. Pruning can be conducted to keep shape when leaves have dropped.

Pests that attack Chinese Quince mainly include aphids, slug moths, and red spider mites, and it may have trouble with rust disease.

Competing for Beauty
Species: *Chaenomeles speciosa* (Flowering Quince)
Age of tree: 12 years old
Height of tree: 105 cm
Container: Round glazed pottery tray
Designer: Zhao Qingquan
Introduction: The Flowering Quince penjing was raised by layering. The third young trunk started to grow later to compete with the original two.

Flowering Quince

Chinese Starjasmine

A twining evergreen vine, Chinese Starjasmine produces fragrant, snow-white flowers in early summer and reddish purple leaves in early winter. It is a vista to see them grow on a rock.

Starjasmine penjing should be placed in partially shaded and well-moisturized environment. It survives well in moderate cold, but needs to be moved indoors in winter in cold areas.

Chinese Starjasmine loves shade and moisture, but it can tolerate drought for a short period of time, so keep the soil damp, but not saturated.

Organic liquid fertilizers are usually applied when it grows in spring and summer, but no fertilizing is needed in autumn and winter.

While pruning and shaping work is often done when it is at the state of dormancy, dead branches or leaves and vines too long or too dense can be regularly removed to keep its pleasing shape.

It is repotted every two or three years in early spring before new growth appears. Remove about half of old soil and prune redundant roots before it is repotted in fertile acid or neutral soil with good drainage and air permeability.

It is generally a very healthy plant and seldom gets into trouble with pests.

Graceful as It is
Species: *Trachelospermum jasminoides* (Chinese Starjasmine)
Age of tree: 40 years old
Spread: 65 cm
Container: Square glazed pottery pot
Designer: Zhao Qingquan
Introduction: A typical vine penjing species, the evergreen Chinese Starjasmine is known for its snowflake-shaped leaves and aromatic fragrance. With long drooping branches, the penjing is as graceful as a lady, capturing the charm of a traditional Chinese painting.

Chinese Starjasmine

144

Chinese Wisteria

With refined dragon-shaped branches, magnificent green leaves and beautiful purple flowers, Chinese Wisteria is a favorite for penjing enthusiasts.

The wisteria loves full sun though it can tolerate partial shade, so it is often placed outdoors in a well-ventilated light environment. While it survives cold weather, in winter you may want to put it in a sunny place outdoors with protection from the wind. It can also be placed indoors.

The wisteria penjing needs adequate water in growth months. Less water is need since August every year to allow the pot soil to be slightly dry to promote more flowers in the coming year.

Chinese Wisteria needs to be fed frequently especially in growing months, but fertilizing should be reduced in flowering period and after August. No fertilizing is needed when the leaves have fallen away.

While unnecessary new buds in spring need to be pinched off from time to time, you would need to perform a hard pruning in winter when the leaves have dropped. It is important in pruning that long fresh shoots may be cut back to keep its shape. Of course, water sprouts and dense branches are often pruned frequently.

It needs to be repotted annually or biannually, in early spring or late autumn. Chinese Wisteria loves loose, fertile sub-acid soil with good drainage.

Chinese Wisteria has trouble with aphids, slug moths, and lappet moths.

Drooping Clusters of Flowers
Species: *Wisteria sinensis* (Chinese Wisteria)
Age of tree: 50 years old
Height of tree: 45 cm
Container: Chinese-crabapple-shaped glazed pottery pot
Designer: Zhao Qingquan
Introduction: Chinese Wisteria, a popular flower-effect climbing vine, produces gorgeous curved branches and drooping clusters of fragrant flowers, forming a graceful structure. This penjing, trained from an old stump, has roots as its trunks, having assumed an ancient appearance. With its stunning blooms in spring, it is like a Chinese bird-and-flower painting.

Chinese Wisteria

Crape Myrtle

Crape Myrtle is an outstanding ornamental tree because of clusters of engaging flowers, which cover the whole tree. It can be as long as 100 days, from the summer to autumn.

Crape Myrtle loves full sun, but it can tolerate shade.

It should be watered adequately, especially during flowering season, but excess water in pot should be avoided. It needs less watering during its dormancy.

A tree with long flowering season, it needs to be fed more frequently than other shrubs with thin liquid fertilizer in its growing months.

Flowered branches need to be pruned when flowering season ends and, at the same time, remove unhealthy branches and biennially dense parts of foliage.

It needs to be repotted annually or biennially, usually in March or April. Crape Myrtle loves loose, fertile soil for its dense foliage.

Pests that attack the Crape Myrtle include scale insects, slug moths, and aphids. It can be easily infected with sooty mould caused by scale insects, which should be frequently checked and controlled when they are found.

Gorgeous Flowers
Species: *Lagerstroe indica* (Crape Myrtle)
Age of tree: 120 years old
Height of tree: 150 cm
Container: Rectanglar glazed pottery tray
Collector: Penjing Museum of Yangzhou
Introduction: Crape Myrtle is an outstanding ornamental tree because of its long blooming season of engaging flowers, which cover the whole foliage. This specimen has been trained from an earlier stump. While the main trunk has only its bark left, it produces a vigorous crown with rich flowers.

Crape Myrtle

Fernleaf Hedge Bamboo

With beautiful shapes and dark green foliage, the evergreen Fernleaf Hedge Bamboo makes ideal forest penjing.

Fernleaf Hedge Bamboo prefers warm, moist places with a sunny exposure. It should be protected from wind. Shading measures are required in the hottest weeks of the summer. While it is cold-resistant, it is desirable to move it to a sheltered structure in winter.

Keep potting compost moist. Water it frequently and spray water on leaves in growing season and in the hottest weeks of summer. However, excess water in pot is damaging to it.

Fernleaf Hedge Bamboo is not a fertilizer-consuming plant; two or three fertilizing in growing season will suffice.

Young rhizomes continue to sprout at

Seven Sages of the Bamboo Grove
Species: *Bambusa multiplex cv. fernleaf* (Fernleaf Hedge Bamboo)
Type of rock: Turtle Shell Rock
Length of container: 100 cm
Container: Oval marble tray
Designer: Zhao Qingquan
Introduction: This Fernleaf Hedge Bamboo penjing features "Seven Sages of the Bamboo Grove," a group of well-known Chinese Taoist scholars in Wei and Jin period (220 - 420), including Ji Kang, Ruan Ji, Shan Tao, Xiang Xiu, Liu Ling, Wang Rong, and Yuan Xian, who lived around Shanyang (present Xiuwu, Henan Province), where they enjoyed and praised in their works the simple, rustic life.

Fernleaf Hedge Bamboo

the base of the penjing in growing months, and they can be cut back when they are competing with the main canes. The theory behind bamboo pruning is that well-pruned canes vary in height, density, and ways they stand. Branches too dense or too weak should be removed.

It needs to be repotted biennially, in April or May. Remove about half of old soil in root mass and old and weak roots before it is repotted in loose fertile soil with good drainage and air permeability, but fibrous roots should be well protected. It is important that repotted penjing trees be placed in a shaded area for a period of time and that the potted soil has good moisture.

Pests that attack Fernleaf Hedge Bamboo mainly include scale insects, aphids, bamboo-moth, bagworm moths, and lace bugs. It may be infected with leaf blight and rust disease.

Japanese Maple

The great artistic value of Japanese Maple penjing lies in its elegant shape and beautiful leaves, which turn bright red in autumn.

The maple loves warm and moist sites with adequate but gentle sunshine, and it is often placed in a well-lit place with good humidity and ventilation. Sheltering is required in summer to avoid leaf burns, but adequate sunlight encourages change of leaf color in autumn. An indoor environment is desirable for it to overwinter.

Soil should be kept damp, but not saturated. In summer, watering it in the early morning and in the evening, as it does not handle abrupt changes in temperature very well. Less water is needed when leaves have turned red in autumn.

Frequent feeding is needed in growing months in spring and summer; solution has to be thin and a high-phosphorous or high-potassium type will benefit the bright color of leaves.

Pinch off new buds as soon as they come out. Cut back new growth to one or two leaf pairs to keep shape, when they have four or five pairs. Branch pruning is performed during the season of dormancy, and one or two pairs of leaves are often left.

All leaves can be removed when autumn approaches and a thin liquid fertilizer is applied to promote bright-colored fresh leaves, which come out in about two weeks. This process also helps to delay fall of leaf.

It needs to be repotted every two or three years before new growth starts in spring. Remove about half of old soil in root mass before it is repotted in loose, fertile acid or neutral soil with humus.

Japanese Maple may be attacked by powdery mildew and pests such as scale insects, slug moths, bagworm moths, and long-horned beetles.

Littleleaf Boxwood

One of the traditional penjing trees in China, Littleleaf Boxwood is known for its beautiful silver trunk and dense evergreen foliage.

It needs a location with partial shade, especially in the hottest weeks of the summer.

Littleleaf Boxwood prefers moisture, so it is important to keep soil damp, but not too wet.

It requires no special fertilizing, but it is desirable to feed it once or twice with a thoroughly decomposed liquid cake fertilizer in the spring and autumn months.

Littleleaf Boxwood grows fast, so frequent trimming is needed. Generally, new growth is cut back to the first one or two knots to keep its shape. The fruits need to be picked as soon as they come out, which helps to save nutrition for its growth.

It is repotted every two or three years in early spring before new growth appears or in late autumn. Remove about half of old soil of the root mass and some old roots as well. The plant grows well in any type of soil.

Although it is a very healthy tree, it may have trouble with box-tree pyralids, and scale insects, and it may be infected with sooty mould caused by scale insects. The best way to keep it healthy is to wash its leaves by spraying water on them frequently.

(facing page)

Gorgeous Forest in Autumn
Species: *Acer palmatum* (Japanese Maple)
Age of (main) tree: 25 years old
Length of container: 120 cm
Container: Oval marble tray
Designer: Zhao Qingquan
Introduction: As a forest-style water and land penjing, several Japanese Maple trees and Ying Rocks are carefully orchestrated in the long narrow container to represent a natural maple forest landscape along a creek, giving rise to a highly dynamic composition with coordinated trees and geologically varied shorelines. The rich colors of the new leaves are the result of removing of the old leaves in early autumn.

Japanese Maple

Chinese Box

Flying Dragon
Species: *Buxus sinica* (Chinese Box)
Age of tree: 45 years old
Height of tree: 40 cm
Container: Round glazed pottery tray
Designer: Xu Ronglin
Introduction: The Chinese Box is a slow-growing ornamental tree in China. The horizontal trunk, exposed roots, and upward foliage of the specimen form a beautiful dynamic composition.

Maidenhair Tree

A unique and ancient species in China, maidenhair tree has a fan-shaped crown, with soft green leaves in spring, which turn golden yellow in autumn.

Maidenhair Tree is light-loving, so it is often located in a moist place with full sun and good air circulation. However, it is desirable to move it to a sheltered place during the hottest weeks of the summer. A hardy plant, it can overwinter outdoors.

Keep soil damp, but not saturated. Check pot soil more frequently in hot summer to see if watering is needed, because the broad leaves help water to evaporate. Reduce watering in autumn and in winter.

Apply base fertilizer every year in winter. Feed thin liquid cake fertilizer frequently in spring and summer when it is growing season.

Pruning is usually performed when leaves have dropped; cut back long branches and thin dense part of the foliage according to desired shape.

It needs to be repotted biennially in early spring. Remove about half or two-thirds of old soil in root mass and cut back long roots of the fast-growing plant before it is repotted in loose fertile soil in the pot.

Maidenhair Tree has trouble with pests such as bagworm moths, slug moths, and leaf-roller moths, and diseases of root rot and leaf blight.

Peaks Envoloped in Cloud
Species: *Ginkgo biloba* (Maidenhair Tree)
Age of tree: 40 years old
Height of tree: 85 cm
Container: Rectanglar glazed pottery tray
Collector: Penjing Museum of Yangzhou
Introduction: This specimen takes advantage of the burls on the trunk of the Maidenhair Tree to create peak-shaped trunk and cloud-shaped leaf clusters.

Maidenhair Tree

Orange Jasmine

With a graceful structure and vigorous branches, orange jasmine produces beautiful white flowers that release wonderful sweet smell. The evergreen plant is most beautiful when fresh leaves develop in early summer.

Orange Jasmine needs a location with partial shade and good moisture ratio. Measures have to be taken to protect it from the heat of the summer and the cold of the winter. It is damaging to it when temperature falls below 5°C.

Soil should be kept damp, but not saturated.

Feed it twice a month in the period from April to September with a thin organic fertilizer. A base feeding of cake fertilizer can be applied in winter.

Periodical pruning is required to keep shape of the fast-growing tree especially in growth months, but not in winter.

It needs to be repotted every two or three years, usually in April or May. While repotting, pruning can be done at the same time.

Pests that attack Orange Jasmine include long-horned beetles, scale insects, and red spider mites.

Light Green Leaves under the Sun
Species: *Murraya paniculata* (Orange Jasmine)
Age of tree: 80 years old
Height of tree: 90 cm
Container: Rectanglar sandy clay tray
Designer: Wu Chengfa
Introduction: The Orange Jasmine has a carefully pruned vigorous shape. The two trunks are artistically orchestrated to complement each other and give rise to a highly dynamic composition.

Orange Jasmine

151

Competing for Beauty
Species: *Punica granatum* (Pomegranate)
Age of tree: 40 years old
Spread: 80 cm
Container: Square sandy clay pot
Designer: Zhang Zhongtao
Introduction: A popular penjing species, pomegranate is trained for its flowers as well as its fruit. The red berries are gorgeous in autumn. This sample from Shandong Province is a cascade-style penjing. The main trunk sticks out of the tray, but the other one is straight and upright, giving rise to a highly dynamic composition with a great sense of lightness and heaviness.

Pomegranate

Pomegranate

Pomegranate penjing are kept for its wonderful flowers and fruit. It is a vista to view the trumpet-shaped flowers in its foliage with dark green leaves in flowering months, while the contrast between red and yellow fruit is stunning in autumn.

This particular tree is light-loving and needs to be placed in well-lit and well ventilated and warm places during the growing months.

Pomegranate can withstand drought conditions, so make sure that you are not over-watering it. However, it is damaging to allow the soil to dry out in flowering months in summer.

Solution of a cake fertilizer needs to be frequently applied to pot soil in growing season, with the help of a phosphate fertilizer to encourage flowers and fruit. However, fertilizing should be avoided in flowering period before it is continued when fruiting season comes. This helps in dealing with premature drop of fruit.

A pomegranate penjing needs to be pruned in early spring. Terminal flowers of pomegranate will result in fruit, so it is important that fruit-bearing branches are not cut back.

It needs to be repotted every two years, usually in April or May in spring or in September or October in autumn. Remove about half of old soil in root mass and prune redundant roots before it is repotted in loose, fertile soil.

Pomegranate has trouble with aphids, red spider mites, scale insects, and long-horned beetles. However, pesticides should be avoided in flowering months.

Princess Persimmon

The graceful persimmon is well known for its long-lasting bright fruit in autumn as well as bare branches in winter.

Princess Persimmon loves warm, moist environments, and it needs to be placed in a location with full sun and good air circulation. Lack of sunlight will cause problems in fruiting. It can tolerate the heat in summer and moderate cold in winter.

Princess Persimmon cannot withstand drought, so pot soil needs to be kept moist, but not saturated. In dry or hot days moisture in the air can be kept by spraying water on its leaves.

A thin thoroughly decomposed liquid fertilizer with proper NPK ratios is applied monthly during growth months to encourage larger and brighter fruits.

The Princess Persimmon responds well to the pruning of its fast-growing shoots. New growth can be removed for better shape and nutrient distribution anytime during the growing months. Pick all fruits before pruning in early March.

Princess Persimmon penjing needs to be repotted every two or three years, usually in spring. Remove about half of old soil in root mass and cut back long roots before it is repotted in loose, fertile sub-acid or neutral soil with good drainage and air permeability.

Princess Persimmon has trouble with soft scales and rust.

Diamondleaf Persimmon

Best Time for Berries
Species: *Diospyros rthombifolia* (Diamondleaf Persimmon)
Age of tree: 60 years old
Height of tree: 70 cm
Container: Rectanglar glazed pottery tray
Designer: Xu Ronglin
Introduction: The twin trunks contrast well in height and dominance over the design, in the same manner that the red fruits contrast with the plain elegant branches.

Snowrose

With naturally small dark green leaves, dense and graceful branches, and interesting short trunk, this evergreen is festooned with tiny, white, rose-shaped blooms in summer.

It is well suited to warm, humid and partially sheltered sites and needs to be protected from the heat of the summer and the cold of the winter.

During the growing months, keep soil in pot damp, but not saturated. Excess of water in pot will result in root rot, especially during dormant season. It is important to spray water on leaves in the hottest weeks of summer, in the morning and in the evening.

Fertilizing should be scheduled to be less frequent, as over-feeding will lead to overgrowth, making it hard to keep shape. A thin solution of fertilizer in spring and autumn will suffice.

While branches grow too fast, young rhizomes at the base of the root can be removed anytime if necessary, but a hard pruning is required in April as well as in October.

Snowrose needs to be repotted biennially in March in the spring. Remove dead roots and cut back roots too long before it is repotted in loose, fertile sub-acid soil with good air permeability.

Snowrose is a healthy plant, but it may have trouble with aphids.

Trident Maple

Trident Maple has a beautiful shape. With graceful leaves, the foliage is dark green in spring, which turns to reddish yellow in autumn, making it an artistically valuable species for penjing.

A weakly positive species, Trident Maple loves warmth and moisture, so it needs to be placed in a well-lit, well-ventilated moist location. Partial shade is desirable in summer to protect it from the

Snowrose

Early Summer
Species: *Serissa foetita* (Snowrose)
Age of tree: 30 years old
Height of tree: 43 cm
Container: Rectanglar glazed pottery tray
Collector: Penjing Museum of Yangzhou
Introduction: With naturally small dark green leaves and and interesting short trunk, the evergreen Snowrose is festooned with tiny, white blooms in the summer. This specimen is the result of years' work of wiring of its boughs and pruning of its twigs.

heat; it can tolerate the cold of winter.

Trident Maple loves moist environments, so keep the soil damp in spring and summer when it is in growing season. A drier soil condition is desirable in autumn when its leaves turn red and growth slows down.

A schedule of thin but frequent fertilizing is desirable in the spring and summer months when it is growing, but no fertilization is needed in the autumn and winter when it is without leaves.

Trident Maple grows fast and responses well to pruning and pinching. Shape can be maintained by removing unnecessary

water sprouts and dense shoots but weak from time to time. A hard pruning is to be conducted in winter.

It needs to be repotted every two or three years in early spring before new growth starts or in late autumn after leaves have dropped. Remove about half of old soil in root mass and prune old and weak roots before it is repotted in subacid or neutral soil.

Trident Maple trees have trouble with powdery mildew and pests such as long-horned beetles, slug moths, bagworm moths, and scale insects.

Clear Water
Species: *Acer buergerianum* (Trident Maple)
Age of (main) tree: 20 years old
Type of rock: Turtle Shell Rock
Length of container: 85 cm
Container: Rectanglar marble tray
Designer: Zhao Qingquan
Introduction: This forest penjing of Trident Maples was a demo at the Mid Atlantic Bonsai Symposium held in New Jersey in 2001, and is at present part of a collection at the National Bonsai & Penjing Museum of America. With the combination style layout, the dominant and subordinate parts are arranged at the two sides of the creek, which joins the perceived "water" in the front of the container.

Trident Maple